CONSTRUCTING HISTORY, SOCIETY AND POLITICS IN DISCOURSE

Multimodal Approaches

CONSTRUCTING HISTORY, SOCIETY AND POLITICS IN DISCOURSE

Multimodal Approaches

TORBEN VESTERGAARD
INGER LASSEN
JEANNE STRUNCK

AALBORG UNIVERSITY PRESS

Constructing History, Society and Politics in Discourse: Multimodal Approaches
Torben Vestergaard, Inger Lassen og Jeanne Strunck (eds.)

© Aalborg University Press, 2009

Cover: Guldbæk Grafisk
Layout: Lars Pedersen / Anblik Grafisk

Printed by Toptryk Grafisk ApS, 2009
ISBN-13: 978-87-7307-948-5

Distribution:
Aalborg University Press
Niels Jernes Vej 6B
9220 Aalborg
Denmark
Phone: (+45) 99 40 71 40, Fax: (+45) 96 35 00 76
E-mail: aauf@forlag.aau.dk

www.forlag.aau.dk

All rights reserved. No part of this book may be reprinted or reproduced or utilized in any form or by any electronic, mechanical, or other means, now known or hereafter invented, including photocopying and recording, or in any information storage or retrieval system, without permission in writing from the publishers, except for reviews and short excerpts in scholarly publications.

Contents

Constructing history, society and politics in discourse   7
– Multimodal approaches

The Frozen oppositional mode   13
Peter Berglez

How the Asahi Newspaper argued its editorial stance
toward the U.S. attack on Afghanistan   31
Miwa Nishimura

Risk Discourse   43
– The Ideological Labor of the Press after September 11
Karmen Erjavec

Asking the "difficult" questions   67
– a comparative case study of British and Irish
current affairs coverage in the immediate aftermath
of September 11
Sean Phelan

Between memory and taboo   85
– On the construction of images of history in Austrian
mass media discourse
Alexander Pollak

Identity discourse and the construction of images 103
– The role of *Le Soir* in the Belgian identity debate
Inge Degn

A quest for dialogism 127
– looking back at Italian political violence in the '70s
Francesco Caviglia and Leonardo Cecchini

Selling Mozart in Salzburg 149
– Multisystemiotic approach
Eija Ventola

Political discourse in the feminine manifestation 169
– Social identity
Dina Maria Martins Ferreira

Constructing History, Society and Politics in Discourse
Multimodal approaches

The papers collected in this volume are alike in dealing with media discourse, but differ in that they represent widely differing approaches. However, in spite of their seeming differences, they all share the quality of being concerned with news discourse and of striving to find new ways of analysing news discourse. On the face of it, they also differ in that while the majority of them are concerned exclusively with linguistic discourse analysis, some with the analysis of both linguistic and non-linguistic signs, and one exclusively with non-linguistic signification, but again, these differences are bridged by their common quest for finding new ways of reading news discourse.

Peter Berglez in 'The frozen oppositional mode' studies media representations of NATO's 1999 military intervention in ex-Yugoslavia, noting that in the dominating discourse NATO is seen as the public entering the private sphere of Yugoslavia with the UN being placed somewhere in between. The leftist critique of NATO is presented as suffering from a lack of argumentative material, and with its emphasis on the defence of nation-state sovereignty, it is given an essential and natural position in this discourse. In this context the leftist concerns for nation-state sovereignty becomes a frozen oppositional mode, since it has stayed the same, while the dominating discourse has been able to transform.

In 'How the Asahi newspaper argued its editorial stance toward the US attack on Afghanistan' Miwa Nishimura notes that the Japanese newspaper, the Asahi was in a dilemma over Japan's non-involvement in the first Gulf war. Noting that although it is perfectly possible 'to hate terrorism' and 'to hate wars' at one and the same time, it is observed that the Asahi changed its stance on the Afghanistan attack in the very last minute, namely in its editorial from October 9, 2001. This is put down to an interview with Mme Ogata, the former UN High commissioner for Refugees, in which she gives her explicit support to the US intervention. And in conclusion it is noted that the traditional, post WW II Japanese attitude towards the use of violence in international conflicts is sliding.

Karmen Erjavec in 'Risk discourse: The ideological labour of the press after September 11' proposes to analyse how risk is construed in a corpus of Newsweek articles in its dealing with September 11, using Bech's concept of risk society (1995) supplemented with contributions from Critical Discourse Analysis. It is shown that Newsweek over-lexicalizes expressions of threat and fear, thereby constructing the situation as both dangerous and controllable. New technology is seen as both America's great strength and later also as a threat. By way of conclusion, Erjavec argues for supplementing Bech's theory with insights from Discourse Analysis.

In "Asking the 'difficult' questions: a comparative case study of British and Irish current affairs coverage in the immediate aftermath of September 11th" Sean Phelan asks to what extent the different scenic backdrops framed the presentation of the events of September 11th in GB and Ireland respectively. His data are BBC's "Newsnight" and RTE's "Primetime" of September 12, 2001. Phelan notes that while both programmes give voice to critical discourses, they come with an official imprimatur in Primetime which is largely absent from Newsnight, and while he observes that it is of course easier to ask politically sensitive questions when the acts you are dealing with do not directly affect us, he also notes that while the discursive positions documented may be indicative of something inherently national, this is not to preclude them from being used to disguise gaps between the actuality and image of national identity.

Alexander Pollak in 'Between memory and taboo. On the construction of images of history in Austrian mass media discourse' asks the question what was the role of the media in communicating the myth of Austria as being the first victim of Nazi-Germany. In the period 1945 – 1955 the media presented Austria as being swallowed by the German Wehrmacht. In the period 1956 – 1970 the emphasis was on the suffering of the Austrian forces in Russia, in particular at the battle of Stalingrad. In '71 – '85 the uncritical approaches remained dominant with an increasing tendency to represent the war crimes of the allies in a more drastic way than German/Austrian ones. Finally Pollack notes that today the victim-narrative has fallen out of use in Austrian media, but that it is still used as a discoursal resource among Austrian politicians.

Inge Degn in 'Identity discourse and the construction of images. The role of le Soir in the Belgian identity debate' sets out to show that the discourse of the Walloon daily le Soir is a hegemonic discourse that is challenged by other dicourses, which it ties to marginalize, her main point being that 'identity' and 'Belgian identity' are floating signifiers, i.e. signifiers whose meaning must be fixed by chains of equivalences and intertextual references. She does this by showing how le Soir constructs two groups of Belgians: Francophones and Flemings, where the former, we, are inclined to follow our hearts, and the latter, they, have embarked on a war of culture. Thus the discourse of le Soir is a hegemonic discourse which seeks to maintain a common identity.

Francesco Caviglia and Leonardo Cecchini in 'A quest for dialogism: looking back at Italian political violence in the '70s' look for dialogic, polyphonic contributions in fiction and non-fiction in reflections on the political violence in Italy of the '70s. The authors note, however, that a monologic tone is prevailing in most of the discussions about the period, but they do find dialogic discourse in an interview with a former terrorist, who on the one hand refers to her former terrorist group as an 'armed organization' and to attacking and killing people as 'armed action', but on the other is able to refer to the actions of her former group as 'acts of terrorism' and 'murder'. In their analysis of a film about the period, the authors note that the victim of terrorism is depicted as being monologic, whereas the former terrorist is seen as a normal person, i.e. as being dialogic. By way of conclusion, the authors once again note that these two examples of polyphonic discourse about political violence in Italy are exceptions rather than the rule.

In 'Selling Mozart in Salzburg – multisystemiotic approach' Eija Ventola calls for the study of semiotics as a multisemiotic meaning-making process, noting that up until now image semiotics and language semiotics have gone their separate ways. Her concrete material consists of the use made of Mozart in selling various products in his city of birth, Salzburg, where images of Mozart seems to be omnipresent, from Hotel Amadeus over shirt-shop zum Moart, liqueur and chocolate sections in the Spar shop, to genuine Mozart-kugeln, of which, interestingly, there turns out to be both a Viennese and a Salzburg variety. To handle this wealth of data, Ventola introduces the concept of semiotic spanning, 'the way of using language and/or images for purposes of meaning-making other than those intended in the original context'.

Finally Dina Maria Martins Ferreira, in 'Political discourse in the feminine manifestation: Social identity', deals with the relationship between the historical space of the objective world and the world created in discourse. Her data is a painting of 17th century Queen Marianne of Spain with its face replaced by that of Roseana Sarney, a 21st century politician who, as the first woman, was nominated for the presidency of Brazil. According to Ferreira the signified of the portrait is <power>, and she shows how the doctored portrait makes the public and the private intermingle by making the features associated with one individual (the Queen) rub off on another (Roseana).

The papers stem from a conference held at Aalborg University, and this is the third and last volume to appear presenting its central findings, the two others being Lassen, Strunck and Vestergaard 2006, and Strunck, Lassen and Vestergaard 2004.

REFERENCES

Bech, U. 1995, Ecological Politics in the Age of Risk. Cambridge: Polity Press.

Lassen, I (et al.) 2006, Mediating Ideology in text and Language. Ten critical studies. Amsterdam: John Benjamins.

Strunck, J. (et al.) 2004, Genres et rhétorique des discourse médiatiques. Aalborg: Aalborg University Press.

THE FROZEN OPPOSITIONAL MODE

Peter Berglez

INTRODUCTION

The purpose of this article is to investigate oppositional media discourse, i.e. the kind of discourse that generates counter-hegemonic processes (in terms of questioning the hegemonic capitalist system). The complex issue here involves the relationship between hegemonic and oppositional discourse, and the actual circumstances for formulating oppositional notions and ideas in a social reality in which the hegemonic order (capitalism) is constantly transforming. If the hegemonic order is contradictory, complex and always in some kind of 'motion', should this not indicate that the production of the oppositional discourse must follow its path and transform as well? For example, A (the hegemonic discourse) and B (the oppositional discourse) are antagonistic and contradictory, which indicates that B receives its identity from A and vice versa. Provided that A is transforming to some extent, the conditions should then also change for B, i.e. B must by necessity transform in order to obtain its identity as B. If this is not accomplished, i.e. if the hegemonic order transforms while the oppositional discourse 'stays the same', we are dealing with a frozen oppositional mode of discourse.

Public and Private

The empirical material of this discourse analysis concerns the media coverage of the military intervention in former Yugoslavia (YU) in 1999. The material is gathered from two European elite newspapers, the Swedish daily Dagens Nyheter (independent liberal) and the Slovenian Delo (independent), and is restricted to the construction of international relations, and more precisely, the way in which the mass media discuss the relationships between the main involved parties, i.e. NATO (representing the military intervention), the UN (the main international political institution) and YU (the nation state as the target for the military intervention).

The media discourse on international relations activates a particular struggle, which can be conceptualised in terms of the relationship between the public and the private. The mass media negotiate with, as well as determine, which institution or interest should be considered as public (representing the 'public opinion', 'common sense' etc.) and which party should be considered as private (being driven by its particular interests and desires). In the media coverage analysed in this study, NATO is constructed as the main representative of the 'public' while the UN becomes a 'semi-public' institution, suffering from the private interests of particular countries (such as Russia, China etc.). The public identity of NATO is also a result of the fact that YU is constructed as a private sphere – repressed by the 'private interests' of the totalitarian leader Milosevic and his administration. In conclusion, the public and democratic world (featuring NATO) is intervening in the private sphere (YU), while the UN is placed somewhere in between this constructed public-private dichotomy.

The media coverage discussed in this study consists of oppositional discourses, i.e. discourses aimed at counteracting the interests of NATO, mainly deriving from different Leftist points of view. The oppositional code consists of the critical claim that the military intervention is in breach of international law in terms of violating the sovereignty of the nation state. Its core question is whether it is possible to violently step into the territory of the sovereign nation state of YU, and to do so, even without a mandate from the UN?

Of central analytic relevance in this context is the interrelation between (a) the construction of the public and the private and (b) the construction of oppositional discourses. What this analysis is about to suggest may seem like a paradox. In the material that has been studied, the critique against NATO (the oppositional code) is not counteracting hegemony but is rather operating in harmony with capitalist hegemonic status quo. What is being examined here is thus the way in which capitalist hegemony operates discursively within what is 'officially' considered as the oppositional code. This is consequently related to the way in which the relation between the public and the private is handled discursively. The mass media cause an implosion of the oppositional-leftist defence of the nation-state sovereignty and the (neoliberal) defence of sovereign, private (home) properties. The oppositional code is consequently an ambiguous matter in this context. On the one hand it is supposed to counteract the power of NATO, while on the other hand it is stimulating the hegemonic (capitalist) interests in terms of 'protecting the private' (the right to privacy, the sovereignty of the individual, private self, private property rights, private consumption etc.).

CAPITALISM AND MEDIA DISCOURSE

As mentioned above, the media material in this study is synonymous with articles from the leading newspapers of the nation states of Sweden and Slovenia [1]. Sweden, on the one hand, is characterised by quite a long tradition of liberal democracy and political stability and is well known for its (social-democratic) welfare model as well as for its neutrality and non-alignment policy in international political contexts. Slovenia, on the other hand, declared itself independent from Yugoslavia as late as 1991, and is now, as several other post-socialist countries of Central and East Europe, heading for NATO as well as EU membership. Even if these two nation states have quite different historic and cultural backgrounds, it is important to point out that this research project also has the aim to investigate the way in which the mass media from two small nation states, irrespective of their differences, become objects of similar structures and mechanisms.

The theoretical and methodological field of critical discourse analysis is the main inspiration of this analysis. The important task here is to analyse discourse at various socio-material structural levels and to interrelate them. At the concrete and empirically 'observable' level, we find the actual linguistic phenomena, whose potential ideological implications are analysed in terms of lexical and syntactic features. These linguistic phenomena must, however, simultaneously be analysed as discursive practices; as something that is part of wider institutional structures (for example, the 'rooted' genres, styles and modes of media production/reception). These two levels should furthermore be related to certain overall structural conditions (long-term socio-economic developments etc.). These different structural layers are dialectically constituting, as well as operating 'within', each other.

The sections The Public, The Private and The Oppositional Code discuss the analysis of the actual linguistic structural matters, while the following section, Mass Media 'Writing' Nationally (On a Media Discursive Tradition) interprets the discursive material from a media-structural point of view. The concluding section (From a Socio-Economic Point of View) analytically integrates the deep-rooted socio-economic mechanisms involved.

THE PUBLIC

The mass media construct NATO as the main representative of the public, mainly from three points of view. (a) In terms of the military organisation's supposed moral and human concern for the Kosovo-Albanian population; (b) in relation to the organisation's self-assumed obligation to uphold peace and security in Europe; and (c) in relation to the organisation's supposed insights into the shortcomings of the official (UN initiated) international law.

Let us begin by looking at the first factor, i.e. the one related to NATO's self-assumed concern for the Kosovo-Albanian population. The official and propagandistic version here is that the YU province of Kosovo is successively emptied of its Albanian population, paving the way for further Serbian hegemony. As the Serbian president is about to 'cleanse' Kosovo from its Albanian population, NATO is left with no other choice – NATO, as the representative of the public, must intervene in YU in order to stop the destructive regime of Slobodan Milosevic. This standpoint is symbolically emphasised in the mass media by the explicit focus on Albanian suffering and the 'human catastrophe' in Kosovo with front-page headlines and pictures of fleeing refugees. This kind of 'worthy victims' discourse is particularly present in the Swedish media, while Slovenian media in various ways are mainly expressing support for NATO (see below).

> "Thousands of Kosovo Albanians have fled the violence and insecurity in Kosovo" (extract from caption, DN 24/3, while the photograph is illustrating refugees). "Too late to save the village of Lausha" (front-page headline, DN 25/3, complemented with a photograph of a demolished Albanian house). "Half a million people are fleeing" (headline, DN 25/3, interplaying with a large photograph of fleeing refugees; of mothers with their crying children).

The second 'public factor' operates as a rhetorical refutatio in which NATO 'puts all cards on the table' as to why the intervention is accomplished in the first place. It is based on media discourse in which NATO somehow 'admits' that the intervention is not only about saving Kosovo Albanians, but also about protecting certain 'private interests' – an 'honesty' which is supposed to improve NATO's image. In the following example, the US president points out that NATO's military action is a good thing, not only for the Kosovo Albanians, but for the American people as well.

> "Clinton: 'Until now, he has spared only a minute or two for the Kosovo crisis, while this time he explained the history of the crisis in a very detailed and wider manner; what might potentially happen if NATO does not take action, and why this is in the US's national interest, namely to obtain peace and stability in Europe'" (extract from front-page article "Milosevic has decided on military provocation against the alliance", Delo 24/3).

The third aspect of NATO's public identity is related to the organisation's supposed reinterpretation or redefinition of international law (the one initiated by the UN). According to NATO, in order to make the world more democratic, one is forced to break the official written law. NATO's public identity is here potentially supported by the kind of media discourse that implies that official law is corrupt, unjust and somehow outdated (and is therefore undermining the public interests). For example:

> "NATO attack a violation of international law" (headline 24/3). "Bring [a voice of expertise, my remark] points out, however, that the right of veto in the Security Council was never intended to prevent political action in local conflicts. It was initiated after the war in order to prevent threats against the national interests of the superpowers//...//Naturally, Bring says, NATO is aware of the fact that it is breaking public international law when intervening – probably NATO hopes that such action will be accepted in the future as a way of regionally side-stepping the Security Council. According to Bring, the possible attack has a good and humanitarian purpose – to tell the Yugoslav regime that its action in Kosovo is not acceptable" (extracts from the article, DN 24/3).

Naturally, NATO does not want to be accused of being driven by private interests, i.e. of being an organisation that is striving for territorial control and economic power. In order to avoid this epithet, NATO is however also dependent on the way in which other institutions and parties are constructed and whether they are portrayed as more or less public/private than NATO. It is particularly important to NATO that the UN and its international law appear as a serious obstacle to public political-moral action (to help the Kosovo-Albanian people).

In the media-discursive example above, the voice of expertise emphasises that the right of veto should be viewed as an old cold-war product ('It was initiated after the war in order to prevent threats against the national interests of the superpowers'), while this has developed into a situation in which the UN is openly exploited by various private interests (China, Russia), which are illegitimately protecting their own 'internal affairs' ('The right of veto in the UN Security Council...was never intended to prevent action in local conflicts'). Examples, such as the following, promote the notion that the UN has developed into this 'debate forum', characterised by quarrels between various interests:

> "Deep rift within the UN" (headline). "After NATO's attacks on Yugoslav targets, a deep rift has occurred in the UN Security Council. This became evident after a crisis meeting in the Council, which was held on Russia's initiative after the attacks. The Russian UN ambassador Sergej Lavrov said that NATO has violated international law and demanded that the alliance must stop 'the illegal military actions'. China, India and Belarus supported Russia//...//The US and its allies, including Bosnia and Slovenia, said that the humanitarian conditions in Kosovo indicate a crisis situation that gives NATO the right to attack without a mandate from the UN. All other alternatives have been explored, the countries stated" (extracts from the article, DN 26/3).

While this could be interpreted as evidence of the democratic and open character of the UN, another interpretation is that of the UN as a 'discussion club' for private parties; an institution that does not take concrete action but rather talk too much and refer to some (old) legal documents (the international law). The more the UN is constructed as a semi-public institution suffering from the undermining and strategic acts of particular interests (nation states), the better for NATO and its public identity.

The Private

The main symbolic support for NATO derives from the construction of the relationship between NATO and YU. The more YU is constructed as a degenerated private sphere ruled by the private interests of Milosevic, the more NATO strengthens its identity as the main spokesman for the whole 'enlightened' liberal-democratic system. On the construction of the private identity of YU, what one should pay attention to is, first, the synonymous relationship between the 'private' person Slobodan Milosevic and YU as such. In this context, NATO is able to take advantage of the already established bad image of Milosevic, created by the Western media in connection with the wars in Croatia and Bosnia-Herzegovina during the first half of the nineties.

> "On Tuesday, the German Chancellor Gerhard Schroeder motivated the possible attack against Yugoslavia in the sense that president Milosevic has violated humanitarian and international law" (from article, "NATO attack a violation of international law", DN 24/3). "Clinton: 'If Milosevic does not want peace, we have to delimit his ability to continue the warfare'" (extract from front-page article "Milosevic has decided on military provocation against the alliance", Delo 24/3). "The Italian Prime Minister Massimo D'Alema informed Slobodan Milosevic that, in the centre of Europe, it is not acceptable to make use of military force against a civilian population simply because it is of a certain ethnic origin" (introduction from article "Fear for refugees and US dominance", Delo 24/3).

The crisis and debacle of YU is here more or less synonymous with the criminal behaviour of one person. By committing crimes such as ethnic cleansing and corruption, this person has transformed a whole nation state into his own (private) garden of destruction: YU is Slobodan Milosevic. Such personalisation of a social formation represents a rather established mode of constructing nation states, organisations etc. Compare for example with 'Olof Palme's Sweden'.

The second aspect of YU and its private character is related to the sphere of the capitalist market economy and to some of its typical (capitalist) practices. In this context 'the private' exclusively relates to the private sector and the strategic handling with money as a social marker. What is particularly important here is the construction of Milosevic as a man of the economic market, rather than of politics, and the construction of the interests of the 'people'.

> "Milosevic wants to become a mythical martyr" (headline). "A person who has got his head turned by his own picture will hardly budge an inch to 'Western rational compromising' [introduction]. Foreign diplomats met Milosevic, a man of the world, who learned to speak English with an American accent during his time in the US, working as a director of a Belgrade bank. And to begin with, due

to his gentle manners, they were deluded to think that they had met someone who understood them. As they were speaking the same language! But Slobodan Milosevic was not a Western democrat, not even a socialist. For him, the membership in the Communist party was only a stepping-stone" (extract from article, DN 26/3).

"Back when he was still a banker, Slobodan Milosevic was about to open his own banking business in New York. The Belgrade Television recorded the event and the tape was immediately sent by airplane to Belgrade. The next day, Milosevic impatiently listened to the evening news and waited for his 'event' to be announced. When he realised that it had been moved to the less prominent news, later in the evening, he got furious: 'What the hell, they don't know who they're dealing with!'" (extract from front-page column "When (not) knowing who you are dealing with", Delo, 24/3).

Milosevic appears as a champagne socialist due to his former banking career in the very heart of the capitalist system ('New York'). The bad image of Milosevic is linked to his private-economic engagements in terms of being a mean businessman. Even if it is pointed out that his business career is in the past, still, the rhetorical point with this discourse is to emphasise that his former identity still exists and that it nowadays operates in the bleeding heart of the YU state. The construction of Milosevic as a 'mean businessman' as well as a person with a bourgeois chameleon character ('…his gentle manners, they were deluded to think that they had met someone who understood them') fits in well with the general media image of Milosevic, the one built up throughout the nineties, establishing the Yugoslavian leader as a pseudo-politician. Due to his ability to easily switch and mix ideological elements in his propaganda – communist, fascist, bourgeois liberal etc. (see Salecl 1994) – what has been considered the essential 'kernel of Milosevic', his 'true' identity beyond all these positions, has been his 'exploitative' side (of the former socialist system, of the Serb people etc.). The way in which YU and Milosevic are constructed, which has been analysed in this section, consequently supports the ideological notion or logic that public NATO intervenes in the corrupted private sphere of YU.

The Oppositional Discourse

The hegemonic meaning (the discursive support of NATO) is however also challenged by the inclusion of critical discourse. In both national mass media, room is provided for certain law experts as well as for Leftists activists, academics and politicians, to express oppositional interpretations of NATO's military mission. In this context the mass media generate a critical discussion on which public law is the most legitimate – the written or the unwritten? While NATO represents the implementation of an 'unwritten law', the leftist-oppositional discourse rather supports the authority of the official written law, i.e. the international public law and the authority of the UN Security Council:

> "NATO attack a violation of international law: go-ahead from the UN Security Council is needed" (headline and sub-heading, DN 24/3), "NATO calls for a new interpretation" (headline, DN 25/3), "At risk of dividing the Western world" (headline, DN 25/3), "Sweden should dissociate itself from the bloodbath" (headline, debate article, DN 26/3), "Accused on CNN" (headline, Delo 25/3), "In search of juridical foundations" (headline, Delo 25/3), "The attack is legally questionable" (headline, Delo 26/3).
>
> "But in fact, a NATO attack against the Serbian defence system is clearly against public international law. – "An attack cannot be sanctioned by public international law as long as the UN Security Council does not accept it", says Ove Bring, professor of international law at the University of Stockholm" (extract from article "NATO attack a violation of international law", DN 24/3).
>
> "As regards NATO's attack on YU, an important element which should be taken into consideration is the question concerning the attack's international juridical foundations. Even though the NATO organisation makes every possible effort to find juridical support for the military action, still, comprehended from a strictly

juridical point of view, it is against the law" (extract from article "In search of juridical foundations", Delo 25/3).

"On Wednesday, neutral Austria slightly opposed the rest of the Western world by declaring that NATO's military air force is not allowed to operate in Austrian territory. 'As air raids against Yugoslavia have not been sanctioned by the UN Security Council, neither is this compatible with Austrian legislation', it was said from Vienna" (extract from article "Unbroken defiance against NATO", DN 25/3).

The critical discourse emphasises NATO's lack of respect for the law that protects the sovereignty of the nation state – including the Yugoslavian one. It is claimed that the military attack against this nation state is lacking 'juridical foundations', it is a 'violation' of the law or it is 'breaking the law'. What is particularly noteworthy here is the unequal balance of argumentative power. While NATO's military acts are legitimized in terms of seemingly proper argumentation, realized through the generous canalization of NATO supportive voices and sources, the Leftist critique of NATO and the defence of the nation-state sovereignty principle are rather suffering from a lack of argumentative material.

The point of departure in the critical discourse is the question Why is NATO's military operation wrong? The answer provided in reply to this is that the military operation is 'against the law' since it is breaking the 'sovereignty of the nation-state principle'. The core observation here is that this critique does not really develop further. It does not transform into proper explanations of why it is wrong to break the official international law, or why it is wrong to attack a sovereign nation state ruled by a politician such as Milosevic. It stops with the spontaneous emphasis that 'it is against the law'. For rather logical reasons this might affect the oppositional 'camp' (those critical of NATO) negatively; as when a discussant ends up in a situation in which he or she is lacking arguments, it is considered as a weakness.

The lack of proper arguments could simultaneously be interpreted in the opposite way; as something that rather demonstrates the socio-cultural authority and strength of the counter-hegemonic party. In their construction of the 'oppositional code', the mass media provide us with the following tautological argumentation. Question: Why is the violation of the principle of nation-state sovereignty wrong? Reply: Because that is the way it is (the sovereignty of the nation state is an 'untouchable' and 'essential' thing). Question: Why is the law right? Reply: Because the law is the law. End of discussion. The irrational and tautological element within the oppositional discourse may be seen as a sign of the established power of the nation-state phenomenon, due to the fact that the matter seems to be rather fixed; 'the nation state is sovereign simply because that is what the law says and any further discussion is not necessary'.

Mass Media 'Writing' Nationally (On a Media Discursive Tradition)

Naturally the oppositional code could have looked different. Rather than the concern for the 'sovereignty of the nation state', other critical standpoints against the military intervention could have dominated the discursive field of oppositional claims. Consequently, the following naïve questions should be formulated: Why did the oppositional content take the format it did? Why did the mass media choose to essentially emphasize the national sovereignty principle?

A possible way to grasp this matter is to pay attention to the relationship between national mass media and the nation-state phenomenon itself. What is at stake in this context is the fact that national identity and the nation state are constituted by institutions such as the mass media (along with the educational system etc.). The mass media is a forceful naturalizer of the national home, constantly 'essentializing' the nation state when cognitively structuring and explaining the social reality (Anderson 1991). It is like a specific mode of writing, characterized by the lawlike routine of separating 'domestic (national) news' from 'foreign news', or by interpreting and explaining 'international matters' from a national-domestic point of view. Thus we are all familiar with journalistic questions such as In what ways does this or that 'foreign' event affect 'our' nation state? or In what ways should 'our' nation state react to the latest developments abroad? etc.

For the mass media to interpret social issues in a transnational way seems rather unnatural and odd. However, the main reason for doing so seems relatively natural – the mass media are consequently deeply intertwined with the nation-state phenomenon as such. They are not only important producers of national identity and the nation state itself, but they are also themselves products of it. Here we find one important reason why the defence of the national sovereignty principle is not accomplished with an arsenal of convincing pro-arguments – the nation-state thinking is naturalised to the extent that it is in no desperate need of argumentative support. This particular oppositional code, the defence of the nation-state sovereignty, is given an essential and natural position in this kind of discourse due to the fact that the mass media necessarily 'think nationally' rather than transnationally. In national mass media, the questioning of the 'existential' rights of the nation state is necessarily repressed.

But Who is the Nation State?

What is discussed here is an important media-structural reason for the fact that the defence of the nation-state sovereignty principle alone constitutes the oppositional discourse. A relevant question in this context also concerns whether this discourse has the potential to operate counter-hegemonically? Does it somehow challenge the actual hegemonic order? The point is that in certain media research contexts it is assumed that one of few available means of producing resistance is to 'think' nationally. Media research based on cultural imperialist theory (Schiller 1972) for example, often considers the global information order hegemonized to the extent that the only remaining analytical option is to analyse the degree of 'domestic elements' in media content (see Riegert 1998). The national, i.e. 'domestic', becomes more or less synonymous with potential 'resistance' and the core question then concerns to what an extent is it possible to find traces of 'national' elements in an otherwise totally colonized and hegemonized media discourse.

This scientific approach could sometimes become analytically misguiding. The problem is that the 'meaning' and identity of the nation state hardly is a fixed matter. The actual signifier (the 'nation state') can easily switch meanings and identities. Whether or not the oppositional code of a 'national viewpoint' is actually counter-hegemonic therefore depends on what kind of identity the nation state is provided with. We have to formulate the following question: Who is this assumed 'sovereign nation state' in the mass media? What specific needs and desires does it express?

From a Socio-Economic Point of View

There are two suggestions on how to politically and socio-economically interpret the connotative meaning of the oppositional discourse in this context. The overall suggestion is however that the defence of the nation-state sovereignty in this media coverage is not firmly related to an 'anti-capitalist', socialist, counter-hegemonic position. In other words, it is likely that it could activate pro-hegemonic structures and mechanisms.

(1) Protecting the Private

The media construction of NATO somehow generates a 'politicization-of-the-economy' process, i.e. the military organization manages to borrow the 'socialist' epithet of being a state-like power with the ambition to intervene in repressive and private spheres (particular nation states with 'internal problems'). The hegemonic code is constituted by the emphasis on NATO as the public institution that actually cares about the horrors that might go on behind certain private curtains, concluding that this is something that 'society', i.e. the 'international community', should pay attention to and do something about. Simultaneously, due to the fact that YU is constructed as a degenerated private sphere – as the corruptive economic playground of Milosevic himself – NATO's desirable role of being a public (state) institution is further strengthened. NATO thus becomes the liberating force that intervenes in the private sphere (YU) and in private affairs in the name of democracy and universal human rights. As the Leftist critique of NATO is poorly complemented with further explanations of the relevancy of defending the 'nation-state sovereignty' principle, the meaning of the oppositional code inevitably tends to protect

YU's right to 'privacy' (its right to mind its own business without any external involvement). The oppositional discourse therefore also potentially interplays with certain fundamental '(biological) instincts' regarding the right of social beings to defend their 'private territory'. This then helps to blur the distinction between, on the one hand, the content of the (Leftist) oppositional code, and, on the other, certain features of neoliberal ideology (its defence of the private property principle).

(2) The Nation State and Capital Accumulation

> "The bill for high losses, which we expect due to the military attack against Yugoslavia, we will send to Clinton. This slight mood for gallows humour could be heard among the salesmen of the tourism capacities of Portoroz. The tourist industry estimates a loss amounting to millions of tolars. Only for the Easter holidays, at least a third of the expected guests will accomplish to cancel their visits. Every day there are further cancellations of tourist group travels, but the greatest uncertainty factor consists of the individual guests (who represent 70% of Slovenian tourism) who might change their minds on the very last day" (introduction from article "The bill will surely rise", Delo 27/3).

The nation state has many meanings and disguises and this is one of them. In this particular context ('The bill will surely rise'), the NATO intervention is discussed in relation to the negative economic consequences for Slovenian tourism, and consequently, the Slovenian economy as such. In this context the media-discursive protection of the nation state is not so much the protection of the political sphere that once paved the way for the modern kind of citizenship (democracy, public communication, voting etc.). Instead, the mass media protect and naturalize the nation state as an enterprise that is striving, as all enterprises are, for profit and capital accumulation.

In Wallerstein's (1974) theory and research on the history of the capitalist world economy, quite a central question concerns why the nation state actually developed in Europe from the sixteenth century and onwards (see also Hobsbawm 1975). Why the nation state rather than some other type of social formation? Without dealing with the numerous explanations that Wallerstein suggests on this matter, what is noteworthy however is that the nation state is mainly considered as a 'private institution'. The nation state is a defined geographical space with distinct borders, constituting a political 'home' territory, while within the system of world capitalism it is simultaneously operating as a competing (private) enterprise. What Wallerstein indicates is that the nation state is one among several other private-economic institutions within the capitalist order. In other words, the rise and development of the sovereignty of the nation state could be interpreted within the logic of the general rise of various sovereign, bourgeois, home domains within capitalism (the private property principle, the private self etc). Then, in accordance with Wallerstein, various sovereign entities that seem completely different or incommensurable, or which perhaps even appear as antagonistic, may rather express two sides of the same ideological coin. The sovereign nation state is mainly a liberal bourgeois 'invention' and so is the 'sovereign private self', while both of them are inevitable 'cogwheels' of the capitalist, market-economic 'machinery'.

The purpose here should not be to wholly reduce the nation state into an economic institution but rather to stress the fact that the nation state undoubtedly has different, often contradictory, functions within the capitalist system – potentially pro- and counter-capitalist functions (see Poulantzas 1978). Provided however that the nation-state phenomenon is successively becoming more and more integrated in the global capitalist system, in terms of becoming more of a 'private enterprise' and to a lesser extent a political-democratic sphere, it is still important also to formulate the question what is de facto being promoted within this oppositional code? Is it exclusively the 'political' dimension of the nation state or does its 'economic', capital-accumulating identity also receive symbolic promotion?

In order to make the oppositional code in the media coverage work in an oppositional manner, it would have been necessary to clarify that the defence of the nation-state sovereignty does not necessarily have to do with the concern for the space or territory of the nation state itself, but that it rather concerns something else, i.e. democracy and justice in a more abstract sense. Due to the fact that the defence of the sovereignty of the nation state is never properly defined, it potentially includes a defence of all various elements that potentially characterise the nation state formation. The defence of the sovereignty of the nation state is then potentially also a defence of the 'private economic' identity of the nation state – as a private enterprise and capital accumulator. What is further stimulated is the ideological promotion of all other kinds of 'sovereign entities' that along with the nation state uphold the capitalist system. Is not the protection of the sovereignty of 'national private sphere' in harmony with the protection of sovereign territories in general (private property)? We have consequently reached the stage where the oppositional code, the Leftist concerns for the nation-state sovereignty, potentially implodes with the (neoliberal) care for private spheres and practices.

Frozen Oppositional Modes

In conclusion then, this oppositional discourse – the defence of the nation-state sovereignty principle – is by tradition and by routine representing and symbolizing resistance in all possible cases, while in reality, the counter-hegemonic and oppositional potentials of the nation state is rather developing into a complex and ambiguous matter. In some particular contexts, the political defence of the nation state is undoubtedly linked to counter-hegemonic resistance, while in others the nation state is rather another private property and private interest within the global capitalist system.

This analysis has then concluded a frozen oppositional mode of discourse. A frozen oppositional mode is a 'mode of resistance' that freezes its oppositional epithet in social thought and discourse even though its oppositional potentials are blurred; even though it has perhaps actually become integrated in the hegemonic order itself. A frozen oppositional mode is a mode that upholds its oppositional epithet and aura irrespective of context, while its oppositional potentials are de facto delimited to particular contexts or particular historical periods. This seems to be the case with oppositional 'powers' such as the 'nation state', 'slow food', 'Sex Pistols','the Body Shop' etc.

[1] This discourse analysis is part of a larger research project of the media coverage from YU in Dagens Nyheter and Delo, during the period 24-27 March, 1999, consisting of 139 units (articles and photographs) – 70 from DN and 69 from Delo. The empirical material is analysed in relation to several different ideological themes, and the selection of the analysed units in this particular analysis, The Frozen Oppositional Mode, is consequently related to the ideological theme concerning the relations between NATO, the UN and YU. Consequently, this particular analysis does not represent the 'whole' media coverage of the military intervention. For a more detailed description of the method and the ways in which the articles are (systematically) analysed, see Berglez (2000).

References

Anderson, B. 1991. Imagined Communities: Reflections on the Origin and Spread of Nationalism. London: Verso.

Berglez, P. 2000. 'Kritisk diskursanalys' in M. Ekstrom and LA Larsson (eds.) Metoder i kommunikationsvetenskap. Lund: Studentlitteratur.

Hobsbawm, E.J. 1975/2000. Age of Capital 1848-1875. London: Phoenix.

Poulantzas. N. 1978. State. Power, Socialism. London: NLB.

Riegert, K. 1998. 'Nationalising' Foreign Conflict: Foreign Policy Orientation as a Factor in Television News Reporting. Stockholm: Stockholm University.

Salecl, R. 1994. The Spoils of Freedom. London: Routledge.

Schiller, H.I. 1972. Mass Communications and American Empire. Boston: Beacon Press.

Wallerstein, I. 1974/2000. 'The Rise and Future Demise of the World Capitalist System' in F.J. Lechner & J. Boli (eds). The Globalization Reader. Malden & Oxford: Blackwell Publishers.

How the Asahi Newspaper argued its editorial stance toward the U.S. attack on Afghanistan

Miwa Nishimura

The headline of the Asahi's Oct. 9. 2001 editorial

This paper examines the Asahi Newspaper's editorial stance on the U.S. attack on Afghanistan. The Asahi Newspaper is a major Japanese newspaper with a circulation of over 8 million. It is known for its liberal and 'leftist' view. On October 9, 2001, the paper published its editorial with the headline 'Yamu o enu gentei-bakugeki' or 'An unavoidable limited-attack'. The Japanese modifying expression 'yamu o enu', 'cannot be stopped' literally, is a common expression adults use when they feel that something cannot be avoided, although they do not really support it. It is an old expression, now used like an idiom. This adjectival expression makes an agentless sentence. The agent, usually the speaker/writer, is obvious, but unstated. This expression implies that under some circumstances one has to act in a certain way against one's ideals or beliefs. It also implies that it is the circumstance that is responsible for the decision, not the speaker/writer. The speaker/writer, through this expression, claims that he/she is not to be blamed for his/her decision. The Asahi's headline thus phrased clearly conveys the Asahi editorial's stance toward the U.S. attack on Afghanistan: 'The Asahi, reluctantly, supports the U.S. attack under the circumstances, as long as the attack is targeted only (to military facilities and the like, added by the author)'.

Japan's pacifism

The Asahi's stance and its phrasing of the headline should be considered in the historical context involving Japan since the end of W W II. Japan has the Constitution which does not allow the use of force to settle dispute between nations.[1] This Constitution was written by the U.S. after Japan surrendered itself to the allied force in 1945. The Constitution made sure that Japan would not arm itself so that it would not invade other nations militarily. The Constitution specifies that Japan establish the SDF (Self Defense Force) for the purpose of self-defense, not a military force. The Constitution states that the SDF capacity cannot exceed a minimum level of self-defense. In reality, however, it is an armed force for its size and fighting capability now (Ebata 1997). There is a debate going on within and outside the government with respect to the possible revision of the constitution. Some argue that the SDF should be redefined as a force in the Constitution.

For ordinary Japanese citizens, no wars can be justified, not just because of the Pacifist Constitution, but because wars cause miseries and suffering to both sides. Average Japanese people think that in wars, both sides are to be blamed. For average Japanese, wars are something in the past, or something occurring somewhere far away. Iwasaki, one of the three organizers for the international conference 'Between War and Media' held in Tokyo in March 2002 put it this way (Iwasaki, Narita & Yoshimi 2002): "Japanese media (referring to movies and TV dramas, added by the author) do not talk about miseries caused by wars that took place after W W II; neither the Korean War nor the Vietnam Was was Japan's

---

1 This is stated in Article 9, Chapter II Renunciation of War, in the Constitution of Japan: Aspiring sincerely to an international peace based on justice and order, the Japanese people forever renounce war as a sovereign right of the nation and the threat or use of force as means of settling international disputes.

In order to accomplish the aim of the preceding paragraph, land, sea, and air forces, as well as other war potential, will never be maintained. The right of belligerency of the state will not be recognized.

war; they were someone else's wars". This statement clearly indicates the Japanese people's feeling toward wars. This Pacifist view, however, was challenged for the first time during the Gulf War. It is unconstitutional to mobilize the SDF to settle any international disputes – the Gulf War was no exception. Why wars? The Gulf War involved the whole Japan in a debate over how Japan should or could contribute to the allied force. It took the government months, until September 1991, to decide that Japan would make a financial contribution, US$13 million.

For a second time, on the verge of the U.S. attack on Afghanistan, Japan got into the same situation as 10 years ago. How should Japan act this time? On everyone's mind was the bitter experience during the Gulf War. Japanese people feel that Japan's (huge financial) contribution to the Gulf War was not appreciated. The U.S. blamed Japan for not sending any human beings to fight in the Gulf War. Japanese were very disappointed when Japan was not on the list of the nations the Kuwaiti government placed in the New York Times one-page add to thank for the contributions these nations made for the liberation of Kuwait (Hisae 2002). Prime Minister Koizumi looked so eager this time to join the international community supporting the U.S. He took a trip to the U.S. to show President Bush that Japan was behind the U.S. all the way in fighting against the terrorists. Koizumi proposed the Antiterrorism Law to the Diet, specifying what the SDF should be allowed to do in this international conflict inflicted by the terrorism on Sept.11. The House members eventually passed the law on Oct. 29, 2001 that allowed to dispatch the SDF personnel to the Indian Ocean for the purpose of assisting the U.S. force without being engaged in combating activities. The SDF personnel were allowed for the first time to use weapons to protect anyone in danger not just for self-protection. This law has gone into effect for the next two years after it was passed. A bigger legal framework to deal with cases like the Sept. 11 incident was to be debated in the Diet.

The purpose of this paper

It appears that the Asahi editorial staff faced a challenge with the U.S. attack approaching in October 2001. The Asahi editorials generally speak out against wars in principle, but this instance world sentiment did not agree. Nation after nation expressed their support toward the U.S. at that time. The Asahi opposes revising the Constitution, i.e., the Asahi is fundamentally against the use of force to settle any international dispute. In the Asahi's view at that time, if Japan supported the U.S., Japan might be expected to send the SDF personnel to the battle zone in Afghanistan. In that case the SDF personnel might have to use weapons for fighting purposes, which is against the constitution. That goes against the Asahi's basic stance. The Asahi was in a dilemma. This paper will demonstrate how the Asahi Newspaper handled their dilemma prior to their Oct.9, 2001 editorial, so that they could find the solution, with justifications, and convince themselves and their readers of the stance they took.

Prior to the Oct. 9, 2001 editorial

The Asahi's stance supporting the U.S. attack, although not an enthusiastic one, is almost a dramatic change, compared to what the Asahi was saying in the editorials before the October 9, 2001 issue. I will trace what the Asahi had said in their editorials prior to October 11, 2001 in order to demonstrate how the Asahi changed their view. I will translate only those Japanese sentences expressing the Asahi's view on the issue. I will supply some English words where necessary in parentheses for the purpose of clarification.

Sept. 12, 2001:

(The U.S.) is likely to start a military retaliation (like before), but a military retaliation will result in a retaliation (from the terrorists). That will worsen the situation.

Sept. 13, 2001:

(The U.S.) should seek measures to cooperate with the UN, regional organizations and its allied nations, without focusing on a military retaliation.

Sept. 14, 2001:

The Sept. 11 attack should be treated as an `international crime`, not a war. The world should unite to solve this crime, i.e. to find whoever is responsible for the attack.

Japan's participation in any U.S.-led military actions on Afghanistan could threaten Japan's fundamental principle in security (i.e. not to use any force to settle dispute between nations as stated in Article 9 of the Constitution). Japan's alignment with the U.S. (to attack Afghanistan) might jeopardize Japan's relationship with the Arab world.

Sept. 20, 2001:

It is understandable that President Bush uses rough language and (wants to) rush to react (to the terrorists) given the anger of an unimaginable magnitude American people express over the fact that nearly 6,000 people were killed or are still missing. However, shouldn't (the president) refrain from hastiness and follow the necessary steps to convince the international community of his intension?

Sept. 22, 2001:

Is it wise to rush into a military conflict?
(We) want the U.S. to make efforts to avoid the use of force until (the U.S.) exhausts all other means.

Oct. 7, 2001:

There is a sentiment prevalent that we should 'go' (i.e. 'go and fight'). It is as if we were threatened with the question of whether we are for or against the U.S. It is almost like if we were against the U.S. attack, we would be for the terrorists.

Some people oppose terrorism, yet at the same time they doubt that a war is the solution to problems. Take Israel as an example, which the U.S. is deeply involved in. Israel has not been able to stop Palestinians' suicidal attacks by means of its military force.

Is this really a 'war' to begin with? What Natsuki Ikesawa(author) has recently said has a point: "it does not take a war to arrest or assassinate a suspect....The destruction in New York was surely tremendous, but it looks like the insurance companies are not going to claim an war-time exemption "

We all know from experiences that things cannot be divided into 'black' and 'white'. This applies to the problem we are facing now. There is a gray area, where it is possible both 'to hate terrorism' and 'to hate wars'. People belonging to this gray area should not be alienated.

There is probably no immediate cure to the problem. We have to spend time to solve this problem.

(We) have to be passionate without losing our calmness and be patient to solve the problem. We should not allow ourselves to be rushed to any actions by the moment's rage.

We can tell from as early as the Sept. 12 editorial that the Asahi felt that the U.S. would use military force against Afghanistan. The Asahi said that "that would worsen the situation", and on the following day, the Asahi called for the U.S. to cooperate with the U.N. and others. On Sept. 14. the Asahi wrote that the Sept.11 incident is not a war, but an international crime, and that the U.S. and other nations should cooperate to solve this crime, not a war. The implication here is that you do not need a military attack to solve a crime.

On Sept. 20. the Asahi was critical about Bush. The Asahi said that President Bush should not rush to the attack, but that he should follow the necessary steps so that he can convince other countries. In saying this, the Asahi used two very common strategies in Japanese to express disagreement with others: First, the Asahi, before expressing their disapproval of Bush, showed their sympathy toward Bush, saying that they understands that President Bush wants to act quickly given the pressure he is under – Americans are really angry and want their President to take a decisive action soon. The second strategy is a rhetorical, interrogative sentence: "Should not (the President) take the necessary steps…?" This is an indirect speech act. It is phrased as a question, but it is a demand made to President Bush. It is not even a suggestion as it might sound. Thus the Asahi sounded quite sympathetic and polite with Bush being indirect, but the Asahi was definitely critical about Bush.

On October 2. the Asahi felt that the attack was coming soon. In this editorial, the Asahi took a strong stand against the U.S. Basically three points were mentioned. First, the Asahi demanded that the U.S. obtain support from other nations in the UN Security Council. The Asahi was unhappy about the U.S. ignoring the UNSC. Second, the Asahi pointed out that the U.S. had not proved yet that bin Laden was responsible for the Sept.11 attack. Third, the Asahi mentioned anti-U.S.-attack voices heard in different places, including the demonstrations held in the U.S. The Asahi quoted its own poll taken recently: more people oppose the U.S. attack than those who support it (45% vs 42%).

In the October 7. 2001 editorial, the Asahi sounded uncertain. The Asahi was still contemplating what position they would take – for the U.S attack or against it. Ideally they wanted to say "No", but they could not. It would go against the world sentiment and others to say "No". The Asahi once again brought out the question of whether what was going on was a war or not. The Asahi did not make their position explicit, but any readers could infer that the Asahi did not think it was a war. Any readers could interpret that because the Asahi did not think it was a war, the Asahi viewed that the U.S. should not seek the military attack. The Asahi went on: "There is a gray area where it is possible both "to hate terrorism" and "to hate wars". This clearly tells that the Asahi's real position was that it blames the terrorism, but it also disapproves of the use of military force to fight against the terrorism. In short, the Asahi was against the U.S. attack on Afghanistan at that time.

WHY CHANGE IN THE OCT. 9, 2001 EDITORIAL?

What brought the change in the Oct. 9, 2001 editorial? I will present what the Asahi said in that editorial in translation. Those relevant sentences are listed below:

Oct. 9, 2001:

(We) think that in order to destroy the terrorist group that threatens the international community, the U.S. attack on Afghanistan, targeted only at the military facilities, the (terrorists) training camps and the like, is unavoidable under the circumstances.

Osama bin Ladin praised the 9.11 attack on the TV broadcast run by the TV station based in Middle East. (He) will most likely continue his acts of terror.

Taliban still hides bin Ladin…In spite of these facts, (we) still want to make the following clear:
1) The attack should be kept to a minimum. Afghan citizens should not be involved.
2) The attack should not last long. The attack should not extend to other areas such as Iraq.
3) The U.S., one more time, should present the evidence which points bin Laden to the mastermind of the attack in the UN Security Council…This is necessary to obtain a wider support including ordinary citizens…

Japan has almost no role to play in the current U.S.-Britain-led military actions.

The Japanese government owes us an account for (what is to be included in the Antiterrorism Law).

The Asahi's unenthusiasm toward the U.S. attack is obvious in this editorial. That is exactly what the headline implies. The Asahi gave two reasons why they supported the U.S. – bin Ladin's statement broadcasted on TV and Taliban's not turning in bin Ladin. But why did the Asahi, reluctantly, change its mind at the very last minute? How did they justify their new stance? I want to call attention to two articles the Asahi printed on Oct.4 and Oct.6 respectively. The two articles – an invited article and an interview article – both called for the support of the U.S. attack in order to remove the terrorist group, and eventually to bring stability in Afghanistan. It appears that the opinions expressed by the two notable individuals in these two articles played some role to influence the Asahi's stance. On Oct. 4, 2001, Prof. Iokibe (a specialist in International Relations) pointed out the necessity for Japan to look at the U.S. attack in the international context. He said that many Japanese oppose the U.S. attack because of the prevalent "national sentiment" that "both sides are to be blamed in wars", and that this kind of thinking is not the norm in the U.N. charter and in the international community. He also pointed out that if Japanese think that they can steer the world according to their old rules in the 21st Century, they are not aware of the reality.

On Oct. 6, 2001, the Asahi printed an interview article of Mme. Ogata, the former UN High Commissioner of Refugees. Mme. Ogata is a highly respected person in Japan. For many Japanese, she is like an icon of the international political scene. Many Japanese people admire Mme. Ogata because they believe that she is a caring humanist who has devoted herself to refugees for many years. Mme. Ogata is in her seventies, yet she is still working hard for those who are unfortunate. It appears that the Asahi shares this view of her. In the interview, Mme. Ogata explicitly supported the U.S. attack on Taliban, saying that hopefully the U.S. will do an effective job in a short period of time. The Asahi interviewer, in response to Mme. Ogata's statement, told her that the Japanese people will be surprised to hear such a view from her, who is a "symbol of peace and humanity". She responded saying that there are a lot of bad people she negotiated with for the protection of refugees, and that the people in Japan do not know the reality. When the interviewer told Mme. Ogata that a debate is going on in Japan over to what extent Japan should contribute to the possible U.S. military action, Mme. Ogata did not question its possible unconstitutionality but she answered flatly that that sort of thing is discussed and arranged between the two governments, two allied nations. Asked about the use of weapons by the SDF personnel, she suggested that if the SDF is just going to be involved in the air attack, no weapons are necessary for the SDF. But if they are going to work in the areas where there are a lot of refugees, they should be armed. The Asahi interviewer concluded that what Mme. Ogata suggested carries weight and is convincing, in view of the fact that she is well-versed in international affairs and has a tremendous experience working for refugees.

I believe that Mme. Ogata' view influenced the Asahi's stance building toward the U.S. attack. Mme. Ogata, as pointed out earlier, is a highly respected person in Japan. As the interviewer said during the interview, she is a "symbol of peace and humanism" for Japanese people. If she supports the U.S. attack, it is not surprising that the Asahi think that they should listen to her. No one would blame the Asahi for its decision because even Mme. Ogata supports the U.S. attack. She knows the best.

Conclusion

Japan is in a transitional phase in terms of its national security issues. It started around the time of the Gulf War and was accelerated by the Sept. 11 incident. Many Japanese people, both politicians and ordinary citizens, have realized that their Pacifist view of the world can no longer be taken for granted; the same applies to journalists. Consequently, the revision of the Constitution is an issue in the Diet more than ever. As pointed already, according to the Yomiuri Newspaper's poll taken this year, about 60% of the Japanese pollees favored to revise the constitution; this is an increase, compared to 44% in 1994 and a mere 23 % in 1986. In this uncertainty, even the newspaper like the Asahi, which opposes the revising of the constitution, i.e., opposes the use of force in settlement of conflicts between nations, cannot take its strong stance against the U.S. attack anymore. For this reason, I want to argue that the Asahi supported the U.S. at the last minute, phrasing their headline with the expression yamu o enu , implying that their new stance is due to the circumstance and unavoidable. The justification for their stance, different from what is expected of the Asahi, is the stance taken by Mme. Ogata, a "symbol of peace and humanism" in Japan.[2]

---

2 A book about Mme. Ogata (Kuroda 2002) came out while I was finishing this paper. The promotional material attached to each copy of the book characterized Mme. Ogata as Japan's "Mother Teresa". I also want to add that Mme. Ogata was the Chair when the heads of states met in Tokyo in early 2002 to discuss the future of Afghanistan.

Recent media studies (e.g. Bell 1998) and discourse analysis (e.g. Fairclough 1995) argue that media discourse contributes to the construction and distribution of ideologies. What this paper examined, i.e. the Asahi Newspaper's editorial support toward the U.S. military actions against Afghanistan, might be an instance of that. The Asahi's stance that their support is unavoidable under the circumstances might influence the Japanese readers, who have been pacifists. Eventually the support in this incident might gradually lead to a support of the use of force in general, in settlements of disputes between nations. That would mean the revision of the Constitution. In fact, the Yomiuri Newspaper says that it was a taboo to talk about the possible revision of the Constitution before; to do so was associated with the right-wing nationalists, but that it is now in the public domain. A constitutional scholar Sugihara (Sugihara 2002) wrote recently that Japan is now in the turning point where it has to choose to remain as "a nation that will not be engaged in a war" or to let it transform gradually into "a nation that will be engaged in a war". By the latter he means the legal framework to deal with incidents like the Sept. 11, which the government is attempting to establish. In this framework, depending upon what is to be specified, Sugihara argues, Japan might end up being engaged in wars when the time comes. He proposes that Japanese constitutional scholars should take initiatives in taking about this issue, openly and in plain language. The Asahi's stance should be interpreted in the larger context involving Japan today. The Asahi's support toward the U.S. attack this time might be the beginning of something bigger; it might be contributing to the construction of a new ideology in Japan at the time of the transition.

Notes

I thank my colleagues Profs. Katagiri and Ineno for discussions we had. Their views and opinions are not necessarily reflected in this paper.

REFERENCES

Bell, Allan and Garrett, Peter. 1998. Approaches to Media Discourse. Oxford: Blackwell Publishers.

Ebata, Kensuke. 1997. Nihon no Anzenhosho . Tokyo: Kodansha.

Fairclough, Norman. 1995. Critical Discourse Analysis . Essex: Longman.

Hisae, Masahiko. 2002. 9.11 to Nihon Gaikoo. Tokyo: Kodansha.

Iokibe, Makoto. "Tero to taiketsu-suru sekai," the Asahi Newspaper October4, 2001, Culture section.

Kuroda, Tatsuhiko. 2002. Ogata Sadako To Iu Ikikata. Tokyo: KK Bestsellers.

Narita, Ryuichi, Yoshimi, Shunya and Iwasaki, Minoru. 2002. "Senso to media". Gendai Shiso 30(9): 49-69. Tokyo: Japan.

Sugihara, Yasuo. "Urei ari Kenpokeishi no genjo," the Asahi Newspaper, June 21, 2002, Culture section.

The Yomiuri Newspaper, Editorial. The date to be supplied..

Risk Discourse
The Ideological Labor of the Press after September 11

Karmen Erjavec

Introduction

The influential sociologist, Ulrich Beck, commented on the situation after the terrorist attack on September 11:

> "The global worked terrorism has opened a new line in the global risk society (Der global agierende Terrorismus hat ein neues Kapitel in der Weltrisikogesellschaft aufgeschlagen). It is necessary to distinguish between a terrorist attack and a terrorist threat ... It is not the risk that is politically decisive, it is the awareness of the risk: What men fear to be real is real in its consequences." (Beck, 2001: 54)

Beck in his seminal book *Risk Society: Towards a New Modernity* claims that the consequences may be as hypothetical, as justified, as minimized, or as dramatized as elite wishes. Where risks are believed, the result is seen in different social, economic, political and legal consequences (Beck, 1992: 77).

One of the consequences of the attacks on the WTC and the Pentagon was the 'Anti-Terror Act' (officially named The USA PATRION Act), signed by President Bush on October 26, 2001. The Anti-Terror Act allows the US to arrest or detain suspected non-citizens indefinitely, deport them, imprison them in solitary confinement and search their home without any or with minimal authorisation. This Act gives the FBI and the NSA unlimited power. It side-steps all legal restriction, as for example the surveillance of communication, both at home and abroad. With the exception of some individuals (e.g. congressman Tom Daschle) and civil-society groups (e.g. Center for Constitutional Rights, the American Civil Liberties Union), the majority of the politicians and US citizens fully supported the Anti-Terror Act (Halperin, 2001; Mayer, Greven, 2001).

What is the role of the media in the construction of risk and its consequences? Beck identifies the media's crucial role in the organisation and dissemination of knowledge about the uncertainties (1992), but he does not conceptualize media messages and structures as discursive practices or media language. Beck conceptualizes media language as transparent, and ignores the social and ideological 'work' of the language in producing, reproducing or transforming social structure, relation and identities in risk society. 'Language is not just a transparent medium for reflecting the ways things are. On the contrary, language constructs the world' (Fairclough, 2000: 23).

The present study focuses on how risk is constructed through media language. Through a semantic analysis of a small corpus of Newsweek articles, I demonstrate how risk discourse was constructed between September 11 and the Anti-Terror Act. The meta-argument of this paper is that Beck's highly abstract social theory should incorporate the theoretical and empirical account of the discursive aspects of communicating uncertainty.

The first section of the paper presents the background information about the passing of the Anti-Terror Act. The second section begins with Beck's positioning of the media within risk modernity and continues with the theoretical concept of Critical Discourse Analysis (CDA). The third section is devoted to the discourse analysis of the selected Newsweek articles. The discussion and the conclusion sum up the findings of the discourse analysis and relate these findings to the theoretical issues discussed in the second section.

Background

The week after the terrorist attack of September 11, Bush administration's 'Anti-Terror Act' appeared before the Congress. Clearly, there had not been time to draft something new. The bill consisted of provisions that had long rested in the files of the law-enforcement and intelligence agencies waiting for the right moment (Halperin, 2001; Mayer, Greven, 2001).

Among the bill's most troubling provisions – according to the American Civil Liberties Union Legislative Analysis (2001) – are measures that: (a) minimize judicial supervision of federal telephone and Internet surveillance by law enforcement authorities; (b) allow for indefinite detention of non-citizens who are not terrorists on minor visa violations if they cannot be deported because they are stateless, their country of origin refuses to accept them or because they would face torture in their country of origin; (c) expand the ability of the government to conduct secret searches; (d) give the Attorney General and the Secretary of State the power to designate domestic groups as terrorist organisations and deport any non-citizen who belongs to them; (e) grant the FBI broad access to sensitive business records about individuals without having to show evidence of a crime.

The American Civil Liberties Union (2001) claims that the Act gives the Attorney General and the federal law enforcement unnecessary and permanent new powers to violate civil liberties that go far beyond the stated goal of fighting terrorism (see ACLU 2001). Over 1,200 foreigners have been secretly arrested this way, because of mere suspicion. Four months later, 900 of them were secretly incarcerated, without having ever been presented before a judge or having had the opportunity to be assisted by a lawyer (de Benoist, 2001: 126).

Theoretical background
Risk society and the media

Beck (1992: 144) speaks about the 'risk society' as that stage of the late modernity where 'the two great forms of security that had remained for people in modernity' (in the family and occupation) are disappearing. 'Now both are in crisis as regards providing people's lives with "inner stability".'

He defines 'risk' as a potentially catastrophic manufactured uncertainty. Cottle (1998) rightly specifies Beck's identification of the mass media as (a) a privileged site for the social construction, (b) the social contestation and (c) the social criticism of risk and society.

By risk I mean above all radioactivity, which completely evades human perceptive abilities, but also toxins and pollution in the air, the water and foodstuffs, together with the accompanying short-and long-term effects on plants, animals and people. They induce systematic and often irreversible harm, generally remain invisible, are based on causal interpretations, and thus initially only exist in terms of the (scientific or anti-scientific) knowledge about them. They can thus be changed, magnified, dramatized or minimized within knowledge, and to that extent they are particularly open to social definition and construction. Hence the mass media and the scientific and legal professions in charge of defining risk become key social and political position. (Beck, 1992: 22-3)

Beck's formulation of risk is social-constructivist in which the natures of contemporary risks are dependent upon the means by which they are made socially visible. They can only be 'visible' when socially defined within knowledge or a knowledge-processing sphere such as science, the legal system and the media (Cottle, 1998). Beck (1992: 46) also defines the media as the key arena in which social contests over definitions, knowledge and risk consequences are played out.

As the risk society develops, so does the antagonism between those afflicted by risk and those who profit from them. The social and economic importance of knowledge grows similarly, and with it the power over the media to structure knowledge (science and research) and disseminate it (mass media). The risk society in this sense is also the science, media and information society. Thus new antagonisms grow up between those who produce risk definition and those who consume them. (Beck, 1992: 46)

Furthermore, for Beck the media also perform a critical surveillance role: 'The hazards, which are not merely projected onto the world stage, but really threaten, are illuminated under the mass media spotlight' (1995: 101). Beck's social theory leads to the theoretical identification of the mass media, alongside the fields of science, politics and the law, as a crucial domain in which processes of social definition take place. His formulation rightly places the mass media centre frame with respect to social claims-making and contestation (Cottle, 1998).

Beck develops a highly theoretical social theory without the empirical support of the media. What Cottle (1998), Tulloch and Lupton (2001) say of Beck is true. Beck's social theory of risk lacks an empirically based middle-level theory of the media, concerned with the everyday narratives of production and reception. But furthermore, Beck also fails to see the mass media as discourse, as 'linguistic facts', in Poster's terminology (1990: 28). He fails to address the crucial question of how risk is constructed through language. Language, both as a practice itself and as a representation of practice, is one dimension of the social, which articulates with and internalizes other 'moments' (material, imaginary, institutional 'moments') of the social process (Harvey, 1996). By analysing the linguistic structures and discourse in the light of its interactional and wider social contexts, risk researcher can unlock the construction of the risk and recover its meanings expressed in discourse.

Beck neglects the contributions of Critical Discourse Analysis (CDA), which is devoted to the 'analysis of linguistic and semiotic aspects of social processes and problems' (Wodak, 1996: 15). The approach followed in this paper draws on the CDA of Fairclough (1989, 1992, 1995a, 1995b, 2000) and van Dijk (1980, 1983, 1987, 1988a, 1988b, 1995, 1998).

Critical Discourse Analysis

The methodological assumption underlying CDA's qualitative approach is, as Fairclough (1992) claims, that discourse is socially shaped (constituted) and shaping (constituting), that means that, discourse is not only a product or reflection of social processes, but is itself seen to contribute towards the production or reproduction of these processes.

In the present paper, I use the term discourse in two ways: as an abstract noun, I define discourse as language use conceived of as social practice, and as a term to describe one or more discourse(s), I define it along the line of Foucault (1972): a limited range of possible statements promoting a limited range of meanings. I do not wish to suggest that discourse is the central feature of hegemonic domination, or that there are no extra-discursive factors, which play a crucial role in the maintenance or change of a specific social formation. But I agree with Hall (1982) who claims that it is, nevertheless, only possible to make sense of the world through the appropriation of language in discourse. Discourse can have the effect of sustaining certain "closures", of establishing certain systems of equivalence between what could be assumed about the world and what could be said to be true.

The word 'critical' is a key theoretical concept in CDA and signals the need for analysts to de-naturalise ideological underpinnings of discourse that have become common beliefs or even 'common sense' and go beyond the description of discourse to an explanation and interpretation of how and why such realisations come to be produced. Media discourse, which is abundant in quantity and convenient in access, would often be targeted as a research object of CDA, because researchers are interested in how the media mask their ideological positions, embodied in their attitudes and opinions, in the way they present people and issues (Bell, 1991).

News magazine discourse may be analysed into two major components: a textual and contextual component (van Dijk, 1988). The textual component systematically analyses the various structures of news magazine discourse at different levels. As a form of language use, news magazine texts also display linguistic or grammatical structures of words, words groups, clauses, or sentences. The contextual component analyses the cognitive and social factors, conditions, constraints, or consequences of such textual structures, and indirectly, their economic, cultural, and historical embedding. In the following sections, the analysis of the textual component of news magazine discourse will be presented.

NEWS MAGAZINE ON RISK DISCOURSE: A DISCOURSE ANALYSIS

News magazine was chosen for the analysis because of its detailed presentation of social events and processes. In her doctoral dissertation on genres in the press, Košir (1987) claims that because more space is available for in-depth analyses and there is less pressure to publish immediately, weekly news magazines do not publish classical news reports, but opt for articles in which the key characteristic is the desire of the journalist to explain a certain situation from various aspects with the help of research.

Furthermore, Newsweek articles were chosen for the analysis because Newsweek represents one of the main opinion leader roles in the USA and abroad. Its target audience consists of educated and relatively well-off people who have an important decision-making role in American and global society. Its image is that of serious, objective and in-depth coverage of international and domestic affairs, often serving as reference on political and business information. This weekly news magazine can be considerate a moderate but left-of-centre news magazine. (Entman, 1991; de Goede, 1996: 329-330)

THE METHODOLOGY OF DISCOURSE ANALYSIS

The sample used in the detailed discourse analysis consists of two opinion articles and eight informative articles published in Newsweek between September 11, 2001, and the week when President Bush signed the Anti-Terror Act. The articles discuss the domestic situation after the terrorist attacks. The analysis does not focus on the presentation of the attacks and or the international circumstances, but on the internal, US situation. A list of all the articles analysed, with their publication dates, is provided in the Appendix. The data for the analysis consists of all the articles published by Newsweek on the domestic situation in the six issues defined above.

This sample seems relatively small and therefore, I make no claims for the generalizability of my findings. The goal is to present an example of how the media construct risk discourse and legitimate the law. The first question of the analysis is what lexical items are used to present the situation. The second issue concerns what Fowler et al. (1979) call 'over-lexicalization as a pragmatic strategy of encoding ideology in news discourse' and lexical cohesion, which through repetition of a word establishes linked meaning (Fairclough, 1995). Whereas this semantic account takes place at a more local level, I also analyse the global meanings (macro-propositions) of the news magazine discourse. On all the levels of the semantic analysis, the focus and facts regarded as uncontroversial as well as the ideology, which has become part of the 'common sense' and is therefore presupposed in the texts, are identified.

Lexis

The first section focuses on lexical choices, lexical cohesion and over-lexicalization. The structure of vocabulary constitutes particular ways of dividing up some aspects of reality, which are built upon a particular ideological representation of that reality.

Lexical choice

The analysis begins with the words of the selected news magazine articles. It is widely accepted that the choice of the words in news articles is by no means arbitrary. It is not the journalist's own creation, but has something to do with his/her society. Trew (1979), Teo (2000) and Pan (2002) in their studies of lexical choice and ideologies, concluded that all perception which is embodied in lexicalization, involves ideologies. Thus, the Newsweek coverage of the situation after the attacks will be studied, first of all, at the lexical level, because the choice of words is crucial in representing the intended situation about the news events to readers, and hence is an indication, whether implicit or explicit, of the ideological stance on the media in general and journalists in particular.

Reference to the situation after the attacks

In referring to the situation after the attacks, Newsweek used different expressions.

Table 1: Reference to the situation after the attacks in Newsweek

Sep. 24 [A]	'a nation united', 're-United States of America', 'renewed spirit of togetherness', 'spirit of solidarity'
Sep. 24 [B]	'war', 'threat', 'scares', 'fear'
Oct. 1 [C]	'crisis', 'alarm', 'shock', 'anxiety', 'widespread concern', 'full of fear and worry', 'the threat to the country's social fabric', 'danger to national security', 'almost normal life'
Oct. 1 [D]	'fear of further terrorist activities', 'panic'
Oct. 8 [E]	'anxious', 'scare', 'nervous', 'threat', 'difficult situation'
Oct. 8 [F]	'epic attempt to establish homeland defense'
Oct. 15 [G]	'fear of another attack'
Oct. 22 [H]	'anxious', 'worry', 'scares', 'panic', 'concern', 'fear', 'threat', 'risk', 'danger', 'normality as possible'
Oct. 22 [I]	'crisis', 'inwardly anxious', 'risk', 'fear as cleanser', 'fear as unification', 'current anxiety', 'uncertainty'
Oct. 29 [J]	'threat', 'hazardous life', 'future threat'

In the first issue after September 11, the first Newsweek article [A] used 'a nation united', 're-United States of America', 'renewed spirit of togetherness', 'spirit of solidarity' to describe the situation in the USA after the terrorist attack. Those expressions denote a re-established unity of the nation caused by the attack. The journalist's play-on-words of the country's name (e.g. 're-United States of America') implies that the country was not proper before, because it was not united.

In the second article [B] with the overline 'After the Attack: Fighting Back', Newsweek's journalists described the situation as 'war', 'threat(s)', 'scare(s)' and 'fear'. In general, the situation was defined as 'war'. Using the word 'war' implies a state of emergency. To describe the situation in detail, words such as 'threat', 'scare(s)', 'fear of terrorists' were used and the situation was presented as a state of great anxiety.

In the next issue, the long article [C] that described the domestic situation, presented it as a 'crisis', 'alarm', 'shock', 'anxiety', 'widespread concern', 'full of fear and worry', 'threat to the country's social fabric', 'danger to national security' and 'almost normal life'. Two different types of expression presented the same situation. The majority of the expressions presented the situation as uncertain and one of emergency, while some of the expressions, such as 'almost normal life', presented the situation as normal.

In the next article [D] from the same issue, the expressions 'fear of further terrorist activities' and 'panic' were used to describe the situation in the US. In the article [E] from October 8, journalist used even more words of uncertainty such as 'anxious', 'scare', 'nervous', 'threat', and 'difficult'. The next article [F] presented the situation in the US as the 'epic attempt to establish homeland defense'. The 'epic attempt' denotes the heroic, enormous effort 'to establish homeland defense'. A new term, 'homeland defense', was invented; the term has a patriotic connotation that every home in the land should be protected.

In the issue of October 15, more information was devoted to the international war on terrorism than to internal anti-terrorism measures. The article about the domestic situation [G] described the situation as one of 'fear of another attack'.

The issue of October 22 once again devoted more information to the domestic situation. Newsweek described it in a long article [H] using terms such as 'anxious', 'worry', 'scares', 'panic', 'concern', 'fear', 'threat', 'risk', 'danger', and 'normality as possible'. Once again, the situation was presented as a threat and at the same time as normal.

The author of the opinion article with the headline 'Facing Our Fear' [I] used the terms 'crisis', 'current anxiety', 'risk', 'inwardly anxious', 'fear as cleanser', 'fear as unification' to describe the current situation in the USA. In this article, fear and anxiety were presented in a positive light as factors of re-establishing the US unity and solidarity.

The last analysed opinion article [J] of October 29 defined the 'future threat', which was labelled as a 'cyberterrorism'.

To sum up, Newsweek used nouns such as 'threat', 'anxiety', 'fear', 'scares' and 'risk' to describe the situation as a threat. The general definition of the situation in the first issue was 'war', which also implies fear and anxiety. Choosing Tulloch and Lupton's (2001: 13) definition of risk – to over-focus Beck's one on specific areas of (environmental or intimate) risk – as 'a threat to one's economic status, home, gendered (and aged) relationships with others, social standing or status and emotional or psychological states', I define Newsweek's words of threat as an instance of 'risk discourse'. As opposed to Tulloch and Lupton's individual conception of risk, Newsweek's risk discourse focused on the collective level. Risk was identified as a threat to the nation, not only to small group(s) or individual(s). Beside the majority of expressions that presented the situation as risk, there were also a few expressions that presented the situation as normal. And furthermore, there were two articles in which positive nouns of description of the situation were used, and presented fear and anxiety as factors of re-establishing the US unity and solidarity.

Lexical cohesion and over-lexicalization

The vocabulary of any political speech community will have a different number of linguistic distinctions for phenomena depending on their perceived importance. This is essentially similar to what Fowler and Kress (1979: 211) call over-lexicalization, which they define as 'the provision of a large number of synonymous or near-synonymous terms for communication of some specialised area of expertise', giving rise to a sense of 'over-completeness' (van Dijk, 1991).

Let me first of all examine the pervasive use of lexical cohesive devices to construct risk discourse. Lexical cohesion is cohesion through vocabulary – through repetition of words, and words that are linked in meaning (Fairclough, 1995: 121). The most direct and obvious form of lexical cohesion is the repetition of a lexical item such as 'threat'. The use of synonyms such as 'risk', 'danger' and 'hazard' and other direct references to the probabilities of harm also contributes to the co-referentiality of threat. An additional reference to it consists of the lexical item 'fear', which includes synonyms such as 'anxiety', 'fear', 'terror', 'uncertainty', 'fright', 'worry', 'concern', 'shock' and 'scares'. The third group covers references to risk-objects. Synonyms of two subgroups of technology were mostly repeated: 'new technology' and its synonyms, e.g. 'new tech', 'modern technology', 'high-tech', 'advanced technology', 'information and communications technology', 'modern tools', and 'biological weapon' and its synonyms, e.g. 'anthrax risk', 'anthrax powder', 'anthrax attacks', 'bioweapons', 'biological or chemical weapons', 'threats of bugs or gas', 'pathogens and poisons'. The fourth group includes references to normality of the situation with the repetition of phrases such as 'normality as possible', 'almost normal life'. References to the new legislation are the fifth group, with the repetition of the expression 'anti-terrorism bill' and its synonyms such as 'legal means', 'new law', 'Anti-Terror Act' and 'anti-terrorism measures'. In these expressions the main stress is on the premodifier 'anti-terrorism'.

The diversity and the frequent repetition of the lexical items show preoccupation of some aspect of reality to different degrees, with larger or smaller numbers of words (Fairclough, 1992). But the question then is: what were the socio-political effects of this over-lexicalization of the situation after the attack, emphasising the threat, fear and risk-objects on the on hand and the normality of the situation of the other hand, and the anti-terrorism bill in such explicit, repetitive and overt manner? Newsweek's over-lexicalization of the expressions of threat and fear co-constructed the state of emergency by repeating specific risks and their synonyms, focused the attention on new technology and biological weapons as the main risk-objects, and, by repeating the anti-terrorism bill and its synonyms, co-constructed the need for passing it among the readers. Beside the risk, the sense of normality was also used to co-construct a controllable risk situation.

Macro-propositional analysis

To continue the analysis of the news magazine articles, which has thus far focused on the microstructure of particular words and phrases, the macrostructure of the sentence, several sentences or paragraphs, is now examined to investigate the meaning of Newsweek's risk discourse. The semantics of discourse deals with the meanings in terms of 'propositions' (Brown, Yule, 1983). A proposition is a conceptual structure, which consists of a predicate and one or more arguments. According to van Dijk (1988) propositions are smallest independent meaning constructs of language and thought, which are typically expressed by single sentence or clauses.

On the basis of propositions, van Dijk (1980, 1987, 1988a, 1988b) works out the analysis of thematic organisation of the news. This hierarchical structure consists of (macro-) propositions that define the most important or relevant pieces of information in the text. Semantic macrostructure is derived from local meanings of words by macrorules, such as deletion, generalisation and construction. Such rules have left out irrelevant details and they connect the essence on a higher level, into abstract meanings or construct different meaning constituents in higher-level event or social concepts. The thematic organisation is directly connected with the discourse schemata or the so-called superstructures (van Dijk, 1980).

In this study, a proposition is defined as an 'idea unit', in the form of a single sentence, several sentences or paragraph. The analysis of some kind of macrosemantics, which deals with global meanings and enables the description of the meanings of all the news magazine articles, will be presented here. I will analyse the macro-propositions of the risk discourse in the Newsweek articles from the first issue after the attacks until the issue of the week when President Bush signed the Anti-Terror Act. Because the majority of the articles analysed are long and also deal with other topics (e.g. the presentation of the attacks and international anti-terrorism measures), this study focuses only the propositions in the parts of the articles discussing the domestic situation, which I have defined above as risk discourse. The close analysis of the macro-propositions enables us to look at the risk discourse in the news magazine as a whole and thus allows a comprehensive view of the meaning of the constructed risk discourse. Using the macrorules described above, the most important or relevant pieces of information in the articles will be defined. This is a rather subjective process on the part of the researcher. However, since a single researcher will do the definition, it is assumed that risk discourse will be defined according to the same principles throughout the analysis. I intend to single out the propositions conveyed in the articles about the same issue in the period of searching for a way of legitimating the Anti-Terror Act.

In the first Newsweek issue after the attack, the main proposition of first article [A] about the current situation in the USA is that the unity of the USA has been re-established. The proposition presupposes that in the past unity was lost, but it has now re-emerged. The presentation of the situation as re-united has ideological consequences. The construction of unity automatically excludes others, who are not part of it. The activities of the groups outside the unity are seen as deviant and marginal. The second proposition is that early signs show that it was business as usual. Two main propositions about the domestic situation in the first article after the attack present the situation in a positive light.

Article [B] presents the situation as the opposite of that described above. The first proposition is that President Bush declared the situation as a war. Presenting the situation as war implies that the USA is in a state of emergency and a different way of state operation than in peace. When at war, the rule of law does not operate and civil liberties are limited. At war security must be achieved by military means. The second main proposition – the USA is afraid of new terrorist attacks – presents the situation as a state of great anxiety. This means fear of further terrorist attacks in general, and the abuse of the main American strengths – openness and new technology – in particular. New technology is presented in the article as the main strength of American society, and, at the same time as the greatest threat to American society. New information and communications technology (mobile phones, e-mail, the Internet), which is not yet under legal control, is equalised with other weapons. Presenting new technology and openness as the greatest threats implies the need for surveillance of new technology.

We are free and open, the terrorists are uncivilised and abnormal, is the next proposition of this long article. By attributing exaggerated positive characteristics to the WE-group and proportionately negative ones to the THEY-group, the journalists construct contrasting social groups and define the in-group and the out-group. In the article, the out-group – the terrorists – is presented as a group of ahistorical, apolitical, archetypal Islamic fanatics with an abnormal mix of capabilities, such as the will to die, extremely high intelligence, patience, wealth and technological equipment which they know how to use. The in-group – the USA – is presented in an extremely positive light as open and free.

In the long article of October 1, [C], three main propositions about the domestic situation are identified: President Bush said that the USA would be attacked with even more terrible weapons. This proposition once again presents the situation as a state of great emergency and anxiety. What is identified as threats? There are no specific weapons mentioned, but in the sentences that follow, the journalist identifies all kinds of threats, from public-health threats and water supplies, economic damage and illegal immigration to biological, chemical or plutonium weapons and modern technology. In this article the threats are presented as total.

President Bush's life is almost back to normal is the next main proposition. When President Bush speaks, he identifies his situation as 'almost normal'. On the collective level, the country is facing an emergency situation, but the president describes his individual situation as normal. How can we interpret this discrepancy? In a state of emergency, full of fear and worry, the citizens of the US should act as their leader and role model. But how can they do that? New law-enforcement anti-terrorism measures put forward by the Attorney General, John Ashcroft, will provide national security. With this proposition the coherence of the meaning is constructed: the new Anti-Terror Act will give the American people their normal lives back. In the article, implicit assumptions chain together successive parts of the text by supplying missing links between explicit propositions (Fairclough, 1989: 81). The reader has to supply these linking assumptions between the explicit propositions by the process of gap-filling or inferencing, which he or she is often not conscious of.

In the next article, [D], from the same issue, the proposition identified is: the Americans are willing to sacrifice their civil liberties for security. The word 'Americans' is used to once again construct a sense of unity and exclude 'them': those Americans who are not willing to sacrifice their civil liberties for security. The journalists suppress the information that some civil-society groups (see ACLU) are against the sacrifice of civil liberties for security. This proposition also includes an implicit claim, a presupposition, that there is a dilemma between security and civil liberties, which implies that the USA must sacrifice civil liberties to be safe. By using presupposition, the notion of unity, and misusing information, the basis for the assumption that the point of view represented is natural, commonsense, to be taken for granted, not meant to be doubted is constructed. The next proposition is that the Attorney General, John Aschroft, vowed to use every legal means at his disposal to prevent further terrorist activities. This proposition connotes maximal efforts, unselfishness and resoluteness of Aschroft as a representative of the political elite for achieving security. The words 'every legal means' emphasise the legality of the anti-terrorism measures. Further terrorist activities in general and new technology (e. g. phones, computers, the Internet, e-mail, credit-cards) used by the terrorists in particular are threats to the national security. The process of gap-filling, or inferwncing presents the new legal measures as a solution to the problem of national security.

In the article in the issue of October 8, [E], the situation is identified as one of great emergency: a terrorist assault with biological or chemical weapons. The journalist ascribes the anthrax attacks to terrorists. The main proposition of the next article, [F], is that the US attempts to establish homeland defense with a familiar friend: technology. The new term, 'homeland defense', has already been analysed in the section on lexical choice. Technology is presented in an extremely positive light – a friend is someone who is always helpful and trustful. In addition, new technology, such as 'sophisticated devices and software programs', 'security cameras', 'smart card', 'bomb-detection devices or 3-D scanners in air-ports', 'Backscatter X-ray', 'machines for sniffing our highways and borders' is specified. The journalist completely omits the negative side of using new technology: the possibility of the surveillance of private lives.

In the article in the issue of October 15, [G], the main proposition about the domestic situation after the attack is the Americans still fear another attack. Risk discourse is still present. In the long article from the issue of October 22, [H], the first main proposition is that the Americans are anxious about anthrax. The second one is that President Bush implored all Americans to resume their normal lives. The third one is that the new anti-terrorism measures in general and new technology in particular will make the country safe. Once again, the words of President Bush call for normal life. The gap-filling assumption implies that the new law-enforcement anti-terrorism measures will allow the US to develop and use new technology that will enable the Americans to go back to their normal lives.

The main proposition of the opinion article [I] is that fear re-establishes the unity of the US around George W. Bush. Once again the proposition presupposes that in the past there was unity which, however, was lost, but it has now been re-established. A sense of unity is constructed to exclude 'them': those who are not unified around the president. The author presents fear in a positive light as a factor of homogenization of the nation. President Bush is presented not as an active participant but only as a symbol of unity.

The last opinion article analysed of October 29, [J], is devoted to the future threat of 'cyberterrorism'. The main proposition of the article is: the next threat is the weapons of mass destruction: computers. After President Bush signed the Anti-Terror Act, computers were presented as a future threat.

The main propositions of the articles analysed show that Newsweek presented a scary situation in the USA. All kinds of threats were identified, but in general journalists focused on further terrorist attacks, such as anthrax attacks and new technology. New technology was first presented in the text as the main strength of the US, later portrayed as the greatest threat to society and finally, shown as a solution for all the current security problems. But its usefulness for society can only be achieved by gaining total control over it. No negative aspects of using new technology, such as the surveillance of private lives were presented.

Furthermore, by presenting the American people as united, by using presupposition, and by misusing information, the proposition that all

Americans are willing to sacrifice their civil liberties for security, the basis for constructing a consensus, was established. In the articles, President Bush implored all Americans to live their lives as normally as possible. The process of gap-filling or inferencing presented the new Anti-Terror Act as a solution to enable normal lives in an extremely dangerous society. The Act will enable the realisation of the magic role of technology to secure the Americans from further terrorist attacks. By presenting the Anti-Terror Act as the only solution to the risk situation, the journalists legitimated the Anti-Terror Act.

In the articles, the in-group – the USA – was presented in an extremely positive light as open and free, while the out-group – the terrorists – were portrayed as ahistorical, apolitical, abnormal, uncivilised, archetypal Islamic fanatics. Such a presentation of the terrorists was used to construct an enemy with unnatural powers, a total enemy and to produce fear in the readers.

To sum up, through textual devices (lexical choice, cohesion, over-lexicalization) Newsweek articles constructed risk discourse, and by using different types of implicitness (gap-filling or inferencing, presupposition) and misusing information, the articles legitimated the Anti-Terror Act, especially its most troubling measures: the surveillance of new technology.

Discussion

The above analysis of the Newsweek articles can hardly be said to be properly representative of the complex dimension of risk discourse, but it provides an example of the media construction of risk discourse. It has, I hope, suggested how an analysis of risk discourse in the media can offer the potential for a systematic and repeatable insight into the linguistic form capable of unravelling the construction of risk in the media, and provide insights that are capable of sustaining and enhancing those offered by Beck's risk theory.

In identifying the mass media as an important domain for the social construction and social definition of, as well as the social challenge to, risk society, Beck's ideas coincide with the goals of CDA researchers pursuing the social process involved in the social construction and representation of social problems. But a closer inspection of Beck's ideas on the media shows that his central object of risk communication – the media messages themselves – remains underdeveloped. To put it differently: no construction of reality is possible without a negotiation of social relations and identities, but neither of these is possible without the unfolding of the text. CDA can help anchor risk theory in a detailed understanding of the nature of media output. I shall suggest (see also Fairclough, 1995b: 185-209; Thibault, 1991) four reasons why textual analysis, as part of CDA, ought to be more widely recognised within the framework for Beck's risk theory: (a) a theoretical reason, (b) a methodological reason, (c) a historical reason and (d) a political reason.

The theoretical is that social structures are in a dialectical relationship with social action, such that the former are both conditions and resources for the latter, and constituted by the latter (Giddiness, 1984). Texts constitute one important form of social action (Fairclough, 1992, 1995a, 1995b). Thus, Beck's macro-theoretization of the mass media as a key role within his 'relation definitions' of the risk cannot be justified entirely ignoring media texts (micro-level).

Further, Beck conceptualizes media language as transparent and ignores the social and ideological 'work' that language does in producing, reproducing or transforming social structure, relation and identities in risk society. Language is not a transparent medium through which established ideologies, identities and attitudes are expressed, but rather actively constructs socially shared representations of the world. Beck does not recognise that CDA entails going beyond this natural attitude toward language in order to reveal the precise mechanisms and modality of the social and ideological work of language. The analysis of the Newsweek articles shows how risk discourse can be constructed in the media by using textual devices.

The methodological reason is that media texts constitute a major source of evidence for grounding claims about social structures, relations and processes in risk society. The evidence we have for these constructs comes from the various material forms of social action and media texts could provide a great deal of them (Fairclough, 1995a, 1995b; van Dijk, 1988b, 1991). Thus, the evidence for the construction of risk in society ought to include media texts.

The historical reason is that media texts are sensitive barometers of social processes, movements and diversity, and textual analysis can provide particular good indicators of social change (Fairclough, 1992, 1995a, 1995b, 2000). Media texts provide usually temporary and short-lived ways of resolving the dilemmas into which people are put by the tensions and contradictions which frame those texts. As this study shows media texts such as Newsweek articles provide evidence of ongoing processes of risk construction on a new, collective level. Textual analysis can therefore act as a counter-balance to overly schematizing the social analysis of risk, and is a valuable method in studies of social change.

The political reason relates specifically to risk theory with critical objectives. It is increasingly through media texts that social control and social domination are exercised and indeed negotiated and resisted. The textual analysis of media messages can therefore be an important political resource, for example in connection with Fairclough's efforts (1992) to establish critical language awareness as an indispensable element in language and media education. The consciousness of how language contributes to the domination of some people by others is a first step toward emancipation (Fairclough, 1992: 232).

The reluctance of the risk theory hitherto to recognise the value of textual analysis is, however, comprehensible given the paucity of usable analytical framework. Discourse analysis can fill this gap. CDA is able to provide the risk theory with the methodological tools to demonstrate the role of media language in the construction of risk society.

Before concluding, I would like to point out the relevance of Beck's social theory for mass communication researchers dealing with the future media involvement in processes of manufactured uncertainty. Beck is right to draw attention to the historically new and potentially catastrophic effects of communicating risk. His risk theory has identified broad areas of relevance for communication researchers; these areas of applied theoretical engagement tend to be to middle- and micro-level, and are concerned with the production of media messages and their reception

Conclusion

Although Beck theoretically positioned the media as occupying a key position and performing various roles within risk society and the communicating hazard, his theory lacks a detailed analysis of how risk is constructed through language. The present analysis demonstrates how Newsweek constructed risk discourse through textual devices (lexical choice, cohesion, over-lexicalization) and, with the use of different types of implicitness (gap-filling or inferencing, presupposition) and misuse of information, legitimated the Anti-Terror Act, especially its most troubling measures: the surveillance of new technology.

A close analysis of the texts as part of CDA, should be a significant part of the social analysis of risk. Beck's highly abstract social theory should incorporate theoretical and empirical accounts of the discursive aspects of risk communication and bridge the gap between macro- and microanalysis of risk in society.

References

ACLU (American Civil Liberties Union) (2001): ACLU Legislative Analysis. www.aclu/cogress/110230j.html (November 1 2001).

Beck, U. (1992) Toward a New Modernity. London: Sage.

Beck, U. (1995) Ecological Politics in the Age of Risk. Cambridge: Polity Press.

Beck, U. (2001) 'Der Kosmopolitische Staat', Spiegel 4 (15. 10. 2001): 54-56.

Bell, A. (1991) The Language of News Media. Cambridge, MA: Blackwell.

Brown, G. and G. Yule (1983) Discourse analysis. Cambridge University Press.

Cottle, S. (1998) 'Ulrich Beck, 'Risk Society' and the Media, A Catastrophic Views?', European Journal of Communication 13(1): 5-32.

de Benoist, A. (2001) 'The 20th Century Ended September 11', Telos 121(Fall 2001): 113-134.

de Goede, M. (1996) 'Ideology in the US welfare debate: neo-liberal representation of poverty', Discourse & Society 7(3): 317-357.

Entman, R. M. (1991) 'Framing U.S. Coverage of International News: Contrasts in Narratives of KAL and Iran Air Incidents', Journal of Communication 41(4): 6-27.

Giddens, A. (1984) The Constitution of Society. Cambridge: Polity Press.

Fairclough, N. (1989) Language and Power. London: Longman.

Fairclough, N. (1992) Discourse and Social Change. Cambridge: Polity Press.

Fairclough, N. (1995a) Media Discourse. London: Edward Arnold.

Fairclough, N. (1995b) Critical discourse analysis: the critical study of language. London: Longman.

Fairclough, N. (2000) New labor, new language? London: Routledge.

Fowler, R. and G. Kress (1979) 'Critical Linguistics', pp. 185-213 in R. Fowler, B. Hodge, G. Kress and T. Trew (eds) Language and Control. London: Routledge and Keagen Paul.

Fowler, Roger, B. Hodge, G. Kress, and T. Threw (1979) Language and Control. London: Routledge and Keagen Paul.

Foucault, M. (1972) The Archeology of Knowledge. London: Routledge.

Hall, S. (1982) 'The Rediscovery of "Ideology": The Return of the Repressed in Media Studies', pp. 315-348 in M. Gurevitch, T. Bennet, J. Curran, and J. Woollacott (eds) Culture, Society and the Media. London: Methuen.

Halperin, H. M. (2001) 'The Liberties We Defend', The American Prospect 12(18), 245-276.

Harvey, D. (1996) Justice, nature and the geography of difference. Cambridge: Blackwell.

Mayer, M. and T. Greven (2001) 'Die USA nach dem 11. September 2001, The War at Home', PROKLA 31(4): 541-555.

Košir, M. (1987) Nastavki za teorijo novinarskih vrst. Dissertation, Ljubljana: Faculty of Social Sciences.

Pan, Y. (2002) 'Consensus behind disputes: a critical discourse analysis of the media coverage of the right-of-above issue in postcolonial Hong Kong'. Media, Culture & Society 24(1): 49-68.

Poster, M. (1996, [1990]) The Mode of Information. Postructuralism and Social Context. Cambridge: Polity Press.

Trew, T. 1979. 'What the Papers Say: Linguistic Variation and Ideological Difference' in R. Fowler, R. Hodge, G. Kress and T. Trew (eds) Language and Control. London: Routledge and Kegan Paul.

Teo, P. (2000). 'Racism in the news: a Critical Discourse Analysis of news reporting in two Australian newspapers', Discourse & Society 11(1): 7-49.

Thibaout, P. (1991). Social Semiotics as Praxis. University of Minnesota Press.

Tulloch, John and D. Lupton (2001) 'Risk, the mass media and personal biography. Revisiting Beck's 'knowledge, media and information society', Cultural Studies 4(1): 5-27.

van Dijk, A. T. (1980) Macrostructures. Hillsdale, NJ: Lawrence Erlbaum Associates.

van Dijk, A. T. (1983) 'Discourse analysis: Its Development and application to the Structure of News', Journal of Communication 33(2): 20-43.

van Dijk, A. T. (1987) Communicating racism. London: Sage.

van Dijk, A. T. (1988a) 'How "They" Hit the Headlines: Ethnic Minorities in the Press', pp. 221-262 in G. Smitherman-Donaldson and T. A. van Dijk (eds) Discourse and Discrimination. Detroit: Wayne State University Press.

van Dijk, A. T. (1988b) News as Discourse. Hillsdale, NJ: Lawrence Erlbaum.

van Dijk, A. T. (1991) Racism and the Press. London: Routledge.

van Dijk, A. T. (1995) 'Discourse Semantics and Ideology', Discourse & Society 6(2): 243-89.

van Dijk, A. T. (1998) Ideology: a multidisciplinary approach. London: Sage.

Wodak, R. (1996) Disorders of Discourse. London: Longman.

Appendix

The following Newsweek articles were used in the discourse analysis. The bold capital letters in brackets are used for citing the articles in the text.

- Newsweek, 24 September, 2001, A Nation United, pp. 4-27. [A]
- Newsweek, 24 September, 2001, Bush: 'We're at war', pp. 28-38. [B]
- Newsweek, 1 October, 2001, Bush's Battle Cry, pp. 22-27. [C]
- Newsweek, 1 October, 2001, What Price Security?, pp. 62-66. [D]
- Newsweek, 8 October, 2001, Unmasking Bioterror, pp. 19-25. [E]
- Newsweek, 8 October, 2001, A high-Tech Home Front, pp. 47-49. [F]
- Newsweek, 15 October, 2001, Bush's 'Phase One', pp. 34-35. [G]
- Newsweek, 22 October, 2001, Anxious About the Anthrax, pp. 32-55. [H]
- Newsweek, 22 October, 2001, Facing the Fear, pp. 62. [I]
- Newsweek, 29 October, 2001, The Next Threat: Weapons of Mass Disruption, pp. 13 [J]

Asking the "difficult" questions

a comparative case study of British and Irish current affairs coverage in the immediate aftermath of September 11th

Sean Phelan

Introduction

There are several reasons why one might choose British[1] and Irish media output as the basis of a comparative study with respect to September 11th – principal amongst them, the fact that both countries have an historically antagonistic relationship as colonial 'Others' and, as a consequence of the Northern Ireland "troubles", a shared experience of politically motivated terrorism. Additionally, there is, rooted in history, the 'special relationship' which both countries claim to have with America (though, for obvious reasons, one relationship is much more important geo-politically than the other). Therefore, in the spirit of Chouliaraki and Fairclough's (1999) blueprint for linking the social, institutional and the textual, the key question, for any comparative study, is: to what extent do these different 'scenic' (See Burke, 1969) backdrops inform the way in which media producers, in both countries, immediately framed the events of September 11th? Based on my analysis of two current affairs programmes broadcast on September 12th, that question is the focus of this paper.

---

1 Notwithstanding the fact that it is also a composite of increasingly confident local identities (Scottish, Welsh etc.), Britain is regarded here, un-problematically, as a single nation-state.

The approach

The two programmes, RTE's Primetime[2] and BBC's Newsnight[3], were broadcast at a similar time (between 9.30 & 11.30 p.m.) on September 12th, 2001. There are several reasons why they can justifiably be examined as a comparative case study: both are part of the broadcasting output of state broadcasters; both mix discussion and reportage as part of a broad current affairs "genre" (See Fairclough, 1995: 56) and both are the flagship – at least mid-week – current affairs programmes of their respective networks. Moreover, they both, not surprisingly, devoted the whole of their September 12th broadcast to discussing the previous day's attacks. Where they differed, however, was in their respective thematic emphases; and what Kenneth Burke calls the "circumference" (Burke, 1969: 77) or "scope of their critical schema. Working within a "problem orientated" (Wodak, 2001: 69) CDA framework, complemented by a framing analysis (See Tannen, 1993), it is these differences, and what they suggest about the particular cultural backdrop in which both programmes were made, which are examined in this paper.

Although multiple forms of semiosis are referred to where appropriate, the analysis is essentially linguistic and structured around two inter-related questions: what is the dominant attitude of both programmes to confronting the question of "why" the attacks took place and, secondly, what mediated images of American power are cultivated by both? These questions are addressed with reference to the whole of both texts[4], but with particular attention to those discursive exchanges, and discursive agents, which most pointedly illustrate the difference between the two

---

2 Primetime is RTE's main, mid-week current affairs programme. The show is usually broadcast two nights a week and typically runs for approximately 45 minutes – as it did on September 12th, 2001. The particular edition of the programme was co-presented by Brian Farrell and Miriam O'Callaghan.

3 Newsnight is broadcast five nights a week on BBC 2. Normally broadcast for approximately 45 minutes, it ran for an extended 70 minutes on September 12th. The programme has several alternating presenters and, fittingly, was presented by Jeremy Paxman on September 12th. With his reputation as a tough, pugnacious, interviewer, Paxman is very much the embodiment of the identity which the programme strives to cultivate. As the blurb on the BBC website puts it: "The programme that asks the awkward questions...Newsnight is interrogative, sceptical and challenging. It holds the powerful to account and is the audience's advocate". See http://news.bbc.co.uk/1/hi/events/newsnight/248099.stm

4 As is common within the field of critical discourse analysis, both programmes are treated here as multimodal texts. (See Chouliaraki and Chouliaraki, 1999)

programmes. I give a cursory overview of the programmes' comparative use of sources and consider the overall findings in terms of their respective "order of discourse(s)" (Chouliaraki and Fairclough, 1999: 58). I also, where illustrative, briefly consider both texts in terms of Burke's (1999) Hexad of Act, Scene, Agent, Agency, Purpose and Attitude.[5] Finally, I ask to what extent, if any, the two programmes can be regarded as metonyms for the "Irish" and "British" responses to September 11th.

ASKING WHY?
Primetime[6]

What is most striking about the very start of Primetime is the ultra-confident way in which the context is set by the co-anchor Brian Farrell. The "act" of the attacks is given a clear historical and geo-political backdrop and situated in a wide – and pre-existing – "scenic" (See Burke, 1969) frame. "And little doubt now that the events are rooted in the tangled troubled history of the Middle East. Tonight we explore the catalogue of atrocities that has marked this cockpit of the post war world and sketch the spectrum of Muslim fundamentalism that seems to have spawned this latest holocaust".[7] What is firmly asserted too is the primacy of the "why" question. As Miriam O'Callaghan, in her introduction to the programme's first report, puts it: "Yesterday's events were *so evil, so utterly incomprehensible* that it seems almost dangerous to try and comprehend the minds of those who perpetrated them. But that's exactly what *must* be done [note her modality] if future terrorist incidents are of this kind are to be avoided". The historical cues, sign-posted by Farrell's introduction, are then reiterated. "If, as expected, Islamic fundamentalism is at the root

---

5   Later reformulated as the Hexad by the addition of a sixth term Attitude, Burke describes the original pentad constituents of Act, Scene, Agent, Agency, Purpose as the "five key terms" of his philosophy of dramatism and the "generating principle[s]" underpinning his investigation of the ambitious question of "what is involved, when we say what people are doing and why they are doing it" (See Burke, 1969: XV).

6   The basic thematic order of Primetime is as follows: 1) introduction 2) report on the historical background to the attacks 3) discussion on the mood in America 4) profile report of Bin Laden 5) discussion on what next/the American response 6) ends with television images from post-attacks scene.

7   Unless stated otherwise, the italicised emphases throughout are those of the author.

of yesterday's atrocities then it's primarily the situation in the Middle East that created this extraordinary anti-American hatred. Brendan O'Brien now traces the development of this bitter Anti-Western feeling".

It is this O'Brien report, more than anything, which illustrates Primetime's ambitious "placement" (Burke, 1969: 85) of the why question. Looked at in terms of Burke's (1969) hexad, it essentially offers up a "scenic" explanation for the attacks, projecting what is essentially a critical overview of the myriad historical and geo-political grounds from which the motivations of specific "agents" to carry out terrorist "acts" may conceivably arise. Drawing only on Middle East sources, the report refers to: 1) the "Anti-American & anti-western economic imperialism" at the "heart of upheavals and revolutions across the Islamic and Arab world since the 1960s"; 2) the violent overthrowing of " western friendly decadent [note the collocation] monarchs and rulers" by people such as Ghadaffi, Hussein and Khomeini; 3) their wresting control of a "new economic weapon: black gold: oil. A weapon used to great effect against western consumers… but in the process dividing the Arab world into rich, those with oil, and poor, those without"; 4) the other "tinderbox issue" about "land claimed by a country-less Palestinian people" ; 5) the subsequent spawning of "militant guerrilla groups", aided in part by "sponsors in Syria, Iraq, Jordan, Libya, Egypt"; 6) the hostility towards US policy over Israel; 7) the parallels to September 1970 (when all four hi-jacked planes were "blown up in front of a worldwide media gaze"; 8) the fall of Soviet sponsors which "left the United States as the lone world superpower still backing Israel" and 9) the legacy of the gulf war (" a new symbol of western power: victory but local humiliation). Tellingly, however, it is the issue of Palestine, intimated to be a symptom of Western complacency, which the report returns to in its conclusion. "When the recent Israeli-Palestinian conflict erupted, and a death toll mounted, it came with a tortuous history – a history not often understood in the comfortable living rooms of Europe and America and it takes a terrible tragedy for these questions to be raised. And often these terrible tragedies make listening to the answer impossible".

O'Brien's report is a complex one, which cannot be reduced to some simple manichean narrative ("of course the Israeli-Palestinian conflict cannot be reduced to black and white"). What it undoubtedly does, however, is situate the attacks in an historical and geo-political backdrop inseparable from the foreign policy actions of the West, particularly America. Furthermore, it essentially provides the frame from which the rest of programme takes its shape. Hence, the programme's other report is also a historical sketch, this time chronicling the rise of Bin Laden back to the Soviet invasion of Afghanistan in 1979 – indicting the geo-political manoeuvrings of the US in the process, (we hear a US State official implicitly conceding that Bin Laden was one of the people "we worked with in the past"). The link to the Middle East is also reinforced, as source Fred Halliday, a Professor of International Relations, suggests a very specific political motivation for a Bin Laden orchestrated attack on the US. "And don't forget, his main aim is to build up his influence in the Middle East". Prefaced by a similar disclaimer to that in her introduction (see above), the question of why surfaces again in O'Callaghan's interview with former US Congressman, Bruce Morrison. "It's always difficult and almost dangerous to try and understand the minds of the people who perpetrated the events yesterday – 'cause it almost gives them a justification. But before I interviewed you, we had a piece here talking about the anti-Western feeling and, in particular, the anti-American feeling within Islamic fundamentalism. That is a reality, isn't it, that America is going to have to address?". Interestingly, the difficulties Americans will have in countenancing these questions is acknowledged by Morrison. – and with reference to O'Brien's report. "Certainly an event like this – as your piece said – makes it both more apparent and harder for these things to be confronted in terms of the grievances. The reaction in the United States is not to focus on the grievances, which people might have that caused them to this kind of horrific conduct. This doesn't get the message across. This gets people hardened in opposition to whatever the message is."

Newsnight[8]

With his customary authority (see footnote 3), Jeremy Paxman's introduction to Newsnight promises his audience a thorough analysis of events. "The questions America is asking itself: how did it happen, why did it happen; and what can America do now are urgent. We shall tackle them all tonight". Yet, what is obvious about the content of the programme, even after a cursory first viewing, is that it produces nothing comparable to the historical reports foregrounded by Primetime. Where the latter issues are broached, however, is in the discursive exchanges involving Dr Mohammad Al Massari, who, just before making his first contribution, is described by the on-screen text as a representative of the Defence of Legitimate Rights for Saudi Arabia (although, interestingly, Paxman describes him, initially, as simply a "Saudi dissident" ; later clarifying the description's highly pejorative connotations. "Osama Bin Laden is a Saudi dissident, as indeed you are – I'm not suggesting that you have an identity of views")

It is in discussion with two Americans – former Deputy Secretary of State, Strobe Talbot (live television link) and Republican Senator, and member of the Armed Forces Committee, Wayne Allard (on the phone) – that Al Massari (in studio) makes his first contribution. Taking his cue from the preceding report – which frames the attacks as partly a case of American intelligence and security failure (highlighting, in particular, the unheeded 1993 warnings about such an attack) – Paxman's opening questions are directed exclusively to the two American guests, who, in Talbot's words, both broadly concur that "it is a rush to perhaps unfair judgement to call it an intelligence failure". It is, therefore, already some time into the discussion before attention focuses to Al Massari, who, with a bang, immediately challenges the dominant frame with which the programme has been preceding thus far. "But let me maybe correct a couple of points you [Paxman] mentioned. First point you mentioned, it's undeclared and

---

8 The basic thematic order of Newsnight is as follows 1) preview 2) introduction 2) report on the "how" question 4) discussion of how and why question 5) report on the US response 6) discussion of same 7) discussion on the British impact/response 8) report on the damage to US self-belief 9) discussion of same 9) discussion about the impact on the global economy 10) a round up of the day's other news and preview of the papers 11) Ends with a collage of World Trade Centre images.

unethical [which was how Paxman described "this war" in his introduction to the programme]. I would say it's declared, a declared war, and the United States is engaged in war against Iraq. So war is on. And when Mr Bush said yesterday 'it is war', I said 'hello, good morning, wake up, it is war long ago'. That is number one. Number two, ethical, we should not go in this ocean of ethical problems, because there are many unethical things going on in the Middle East….Iraq". Subsequently, in response to a tersely put question from Paxman ("would you like to explain to us what you imagine these, we assume, young men thought they were achieving?") he outlines, à la Primetime, some of the "scenic" grounds for action. "Oh, they, they feel they are engaged in war against the United States, which is involved in war activities, direct war activities in Iraq, and supporting, unlimitedly, Israel – in past, and future and now. ... So they're full of rage, full of anger, and full of feeling that they are completely justified to counteract the act of war of the United States by their own."

Not surprisingly, perhaps, Al Massari's temperate rhetoric meets with a cool reaction from the other three participants. Paxman abruptly interjects at one stage to ask him "are you trying to justify this"?. But what is even more revealing is the way in which the putatively neutral host redirects Al Massari's comments to Allard. "Sen Allard, when you hear that point of view expressed, I mean it may baffle [animated by Paxman's facial and hand wringing signifiers], it may baffle us in the West, but when you hear it expressed like that how do you think a country goes about dealing with that sort of threat?" Allard, for his part, essentially glosses over the implications of Al Massari's critique and offers instead a stock in trade neo-Conservative explanation for the attacks. "America never viewed it was at war with anybody. And ah, you know, we do realise that there are some people that hate America, they hate freedom and hate our prosperity". The most acerbic reaction, though, comes from Talbot. "I found what was said by your guest in London to be nothing short of grotesque in many ways and perhaps at another time we can delve into those areas, which he calls dark areas of ethics, and I think he has not shed much light there".

Mediated images of American power
Primetime

Primetime, as we've seen, frames the attacks as the outcome – or at least the by-product – of, inter alia, American foreign policy actions. Consequently, the image of American power mediated throughout the programme (often in subtle, lexical ways) is rather critical. For instance, Callaghan in her interview with Morrison, emphasises the need for "maturity" in any US retaliation – the clear implication being that what she calls the "appetite for a strike back" might force a distinctly immature response. Establishment paranoia is suggested too, when Halliday alludes to the "people in America who think they need a threat" and their "baloney" about "National Missile Defence" . Indeed, even some of the more benign allusions to the US are carefully distanced. "Since the Oslo Peace Accords of 1993, the United States has portrayed itself as increasingly even-handed".

The most revealing impressions, however, are those which underpin the discussion at the very end of the programme. Billed as a discussion on the official American response – and prefaced by a brief clip of Colin Powell maintaining that "we got to respond as if it is a war – co-anchor Farrell is joined by Ronan Fanning, a Professor of Modern History at University College Dublin, and Fintan O'Toole, the Irish Times columnist. The image of America power, evoked by both, certainly isn't flattering. Bolstered by a sharp historical parallel, Fanning suggests high ranking ignorance about the tactics of the attackers. "President Bush spoke about, he spoke about 'enemies in the shadows', he spoke about 'their not standing up and fighting'. And in a way it struck me as being very sad, because this was the kind of rhetoric that you got from the British at the time of the war of independence in 1919-21, and it was almost as if he didn't understand the concept of guerrilla war, and that is very, I think, disturbing". O'Toole is concerned about the dangers of American unilateralism. "But what's worrying is when you see someone like Colin Powell, who is a moderating force there, talking about whether it's legal or not. They're talking about setting aside the framework of international law, in terms of the way this might be dealt with. [and with animated confidence asserts] And we know what happens. The military then is given the power to conduct the war and it does so in a way which does not have a great deal of concern for civilian casualties". He is worried too about the American political establishment's swift deployment of an irrational war rhetoric. "The act which happened was an act of war. The way to deal with that act can not rationally be war in any meaningful sense. The difficulty I think we all face now, is that there's a move towards a kind of rhetoric, which is talking about good and evil, which George Bush was talking about, a war between good and evil; a war between civilization and barbarism. .... It's the kind of rhetoric which leads to absolutely, crazy actions". Finally, cued by Farrell's last question – "are Americans going to demand that their [Farrell's emphasis] Government take action against the people who attacked them [ditto] in their homeland" – they both end the discussion on an ominous note, more anxious about the implications of American retaliatory action than anything else. "The American political establishment is moving in rhetoric now, but I think in actuality very quickly towards a feeling that there has to be, not just a retaliation, but a retaliation which somehow is of the same scale as the evil which was done yesterday. And that is scary", asserts O'Toole. To which Fanning adds : "and we're going to see horrors beyond anything we've imagined in terms of the casualties, and the number of casualties".

These discursive strands are not the only ones to be found in the programme. Morrison, for one, is nowhere near as critical of America. Yet, even his contribution – the most significant American one by far – sits easily within the overall frame of the programme; a point later observed by Fanning: "I thought the Bruce Morrison interview was very interesting. But what people should realise is that Bruce Morrison knows the Irish situation, knows the terrorist, guerrilla situation very well. And he is untypical… and does not represent the instincts of the Average American".

Newsnight

Newsnight's clear identification with America, or, more precisely, the perspective of an American political elite, is evident from the very outset of the programme. Opening with the voice and image of Bush describing the attacks as "acts of war", the programme immediately moves to a Paxman voice-over: "perhaps they are, but how do you fight a stateless, faceless enemy?". This is then followed by the introduction proper, where Paxman asserts: "Today, we are all Americans was the way the Belgian Prime Minister put it". More generally, there is the American-centric focus of the programme's reports – exemplified by the report, and subsequent discussion, about the impact of the attacks on US self belief. Hence, as with the geo-political and historical "placement" (See Burke 1969: 85)) of the why question, the only significant critique of American power is articulated by Al Massari. Prompted by Talbot's note of caution ("I think that one of the most dangerous things that could happen here is that both the incident itself, and its aftermath, could widen the split between the Islamic world and the rest of the world"), Al Massari's characterisation of America's foreign policy is again rather trenchant. The "split is already there. It's widening. Look at Pakistan, which was subservient and obedient to America for so many years.... and then now spat in the face and abandoned by America. America is flirting with India. Completely! The Kashmir issue, America said clearly that the United Nations resolution concerning Kashmir is just theoretical. Be practical, forget about Kashmir, that's why – the reason people are demonstrating on the streets [a reference to images of street protests in the preceding report]. ....There are some diseases there. Either these Pakistanis are all full idiots…or there is a fundamental disease which has to be cured. And [with his eyes focused clearly on the televisual image of Talbot] I think if people start becoming rational and thinking, instead of muscle flexing. Nobody doubt that the United States has the biggest muscles on Earth. It does! But… does it have one of the good brains and hearts on head. That's the issue". (significantly, the particular discussion ends there, so none of this contribution is actually fed back into the discursive exchanges).

Admittedly, geo-political issues, of pressing, immediate concern, are considered by some of the other, mainly American (see below), contributors. These exchanges may sometimes suggest traces of the Primetime and Al Massari critical discourses (one reporter, for example, notes the

Labour back-bench concern – which "isn't coming from what you might term the usual suspects: the hard left" – about Blair giving Bush a "blank cheque"), but the dominant characterisation of American power is markedly different. Indeed, notwithstanding his firm rebuttal of Al Massari, Talbot concedes that the Middle East is part of the "scenic" (See Burke 1969) backdrop to the attacks. Yet the image of American intervention is essentially self congratulatory "But, I do think, that precisely because the United States of America had been on the front-line of the search for peace, and has, overall, been a indisputable force for peace in the Arab-Israeli conflict, it will be important for the Bush administration as it calibrates its response to this outrage to take account of the implications of its response for the Middle East peace process." And, curiously, even when there are openings to a more critical discourse (Talbot, for instance, makes several oblique allusions to the possibility of unilateral military action: "If the United States in coalition or on its own"....), the potential goes unexplored by Paxman.

ORDERS OF DISCOURSE

What this study is not trying to suggest is that there is some wholesale difference in the range of discourses featuring in both programmes. In fact, one could say that the critical "discursive strands" (Jager, 2001:47) foregrounded in Primetime are articulated, even more caustically, in Newsnight. Additionally, one could conceivably find isolated moments of local incoherence (Van Dijk: 1998: 36) in both texts, which might seem to belie the analysis presented in this paper. What is important, however, is the place of these critical discourses within the overall hierarchy, or order, of discourse presented in both programmes. (See Chouliaraki and Fairclough, 1999: 58). In this regard, two key observations can be made. Firstly, as outlined in Table One (see below), there is the palpable difference in both programmes' use of sources or agency. Which suggests two things: that Newsnight is bound, as a result, to be much more American-centric and much less attentive to Arab/Islamic perceptions than Primetime. Secondly, critical discourses percolate the whole structure of the Primetime programme, whereas, for a kindred perspective, Newsnight relies nearly exclusively on the contribution of Al Massari – the programme's sole Arab/Islamic source – whose stance, as we've seen, is regarded with some scepticism, if not hostility, by the other discursive participants. In other words, Primetime offers a "scenic" (See Burke, 1969) diagnosis, which, in the case of Newsnight, is inextricably bound to the contribution of one unrepresentative discursive "agent", Al Massari. Our conclusion, therefore, is that, while both programmes give voice to critical discourses, they come with an official imprimatur from Primetime, an inherent legitimacy, which is largely absent from Newsnight.

Table 1 – List of outside sources[9]

Identity	Newsnight[10]	Primetime[11]
American	14	4
British	6	1
Irish	1	2
Arab/Islamic	1	4
Total	22	11

---

9 By outside sources, I mean all those individuals, not including presenters or reporters, who made a discursive contribution on screen – either as part of a report or though direct participation in a studio discussion.

10 The full list of Newsnight sources is as follows: George Bush, Dr. Marvin Cetron (US Government advisor), Neil Herman (FBI), John Ashcroft, Senator Wayne Allard, Strobe Talbott, Bruce Hoffman (Terrorism expert with the Rand Corporation), Warren Hoge (New York Times), Rudolph Giullani (Mayor of New York), unidentified priest, unidentified TV news anchor, unidentified police officer, Philip Lader (former US ambassador to UK) Stryker McGuire (Newsweek), (14 American); Philip Baum (Aviation security journalist), Professor Ed Gallea, Lord Renwick (former British ambassador to Washington), , Tony Blair, David Buick (Cantor Fitzgerald), Mark Oliver (survivor) (6 British);Dr. Mohammed Al Massari (one Arab/Islamic); unidentified victim's relative (one Irish).

11 The full list of Primetime sources is as follows: Bruce Morrison, Ricahrd Hoagland (US State Department Official), George Bush and Colin Powell (4 American); Professor Fred Halliday (1 British); Fintan O'Toole, Professor Ronan Fanning (2 Irish); Mahmod Al Azaahar (Hamas representative),Jhassan Khatib (Director of Jerusalem Media and Communications Centre), Hazhir Teimourian (Middle East analyst) and Sher Mohammed Stenakzai, Deputy Minister for Health with the Taliban (4 Arab/Islamic).

Discourse as a mirror of the social

This analysis necessitates one obvious disclaimer. I am not suggesting that both programmes should be read as sweeping metonyms for the way in which the British and Irish media reacted to September 11th. Any such inference would be much too simplistic[12]. The question I am interested in instead is to what extent both texts can be read as the product of their respective cultural, and nation-state, backdrops? Several observations can be made in this regard. Given its foregrounding of the Palestinian issue, one can certainly read Primetime's historical frame as the product of a political culture with a first-hand experience of the complex, "scenic" reasons for terrorist actions (as is most obviously suggested by Fanning's allusion to the Irish war of Independence). It can also be viewed as the discursive "material" (Chouliaraki and Fairclough, 1999: 62) of a militarily neutral culture which, drawing on its own colonial memory, has an inherently sceptical attitude towards the intentions and motives of imperial power. In contrast, Newsnight takes a much more ahistorical view; effectively deflecting attention from antecedent political "acts", involving both Britain and the US, as possible "scenic" grounds of motivation (fittingly, Paxman's only historical allusions are to Pearl Harbor and the US Civil War). Instead, its hegemonic frame is that of easy, and uncritical, identification with political power, which can be interpreted as both a legacy of Britain's own imperial past, as well as a corollary imperative of its extant "special relationship" with the US.

Yet, I suggest, there is a more immediate explanation too, inextricably linked to the post-attacks' political context. Which is this: to an American political establishment seeking to mobilise international support in the immediate aftermath, Britain – for obvious geo-political reasons – is clearly a much more important political, and media, constituency than Ireland (the number of American discursive agents willing to make themselves available for the Newsnight broadcast is arguably itself evidence of that).

---

12 One only has to consider the polemical warfare in the British printed media between the so called "Guardianistas" and the rest (See The Guardian, Sept. 24th, 2001) and, in an Irish context, the efforts of the Sunday Independent, Ireland's largest selling Sunday newspaper, to lampoon the "anti-American" stance of commentators like Fintan O'Toole, whom – in an allusion to the journalist Robert Fisk – the paper dubbed Fintan "McFisk".

Similarly, one would expect the Newsnight text, as an informal barometer of the British public mood, produced by the BBC, to attract much more interest from an audience of American political observers – as well as, more obviously, British supporters of the Anglo-American alliance – than anything broadcast on RTE. The speculative question, therefore, is this: to what extent, either subconsciously or consciously, do the sensitivities of this acute political backdrop, and plausible geo-political attention, inhibit (but not in some overt, heavy handed way), and structure, the framing of events ultimately presented by the Newsnight production team? Or to put it another way: to what extent do the exigencies of the political "field" (Bourdieu, 1977: 143) self-censor and pre-determine, as Chouliaraki and Fairclough suggest they do (1999: 115), the "order of discourse" in both programmes?

Our view is that the three tiered link between the textual, institutional and the social (Fairclough 1995: 16) is very different in both media contexts, and that the institutional wariness of the BBC to offend American sensibilities cannot be understood without reference to the broader geo-political scene in which the British – and not the Irish – state is a significant player. In that context, I suggest the hostile reaction to Question Time, a BBC programme broadcast later in the same week which was heavily criticised for the "Anti-American" line assumed by many Muslim members of its audience, was certainly indicative. As was the subsequent BBC retraction. A senior BBC executive admitted the programme "went awry". A BBC spokesman said: "The right issues were discussed and a broad range of opinions were aired – many supporting the USA. We did not set out to cause offence but we recognise some viewers were taken aback by the programme and regret any offence caused." (The Independent, September 15th 2001)

Conclusion

This paper has shown how two programmes, broadcast by the British and Irish state broadcaster, took markedly different attitudes towards critically framing the September 11th attacks on America. One obvious conclusion

– for those who view the attacks as "acts" with historical and geo-political antecedents – is that what is posited here as the Irish perspective has certainly more to redeem it. Yet, I would suggest there are other ways of interpreting these findings too, that at least challenge the easy, and perhaps complacent, conclusion that, because of its own colonial experience and history, the Irish state is somehow inherently disposed towards confronting, in sophisticated ways, the structural reasons for terrorist action. For it needs to be acknowledged that Ireland was also the state which, until recently, strictly imposed the so called Section 31 provision: a measure, introduced in the 1970s, which banned all radio and television interviews with political representatives linked to Republican paramilitary groups and which no political party sought to remove – despite the need to annually renew the directive – during the worst years of the troubles (See Horgan, 2001: 149). This begs a more fundamental question: is it both structurally[13] and emotionally easier for broadcasters to ask the "difficult" questions, rationalize the reasons for terrorism, avoid self-censorship, when those terrorist "acts" don't directly effect "us"[14]?

There is another, more subtle, reading of the Irish perspective too, one cognisant of the way in which putatively progressive discourses can be "appropriated" (See Chouliaraki and Fairclough, 1999: 45) to serve paradoxical political and economic ends. For any assumptions about Irish political culture, based on our analysis, need to take heed of the way in which these (culturally accessible) discourses can also function as discursive poses or accessories. Indeed, if one wants to illustrate the opportunistic nature of this discursive "hybridity" (ibid: 14), where better to look than the post-September 11th manoeuvrings of the Irish Prime Minister, Bertie Ahern, who, after stopping off at the White House for the traditional St. Patrick's day greeting with President Bush – afterwards reportedly telling the Irish Times that "Ireland wholeheartedly supported the US campaign against terrorism"(The Irish Times, March 14th, 2002), headed straight for the

---

13 I say structurally, because Section 31 was consistently opposed by large numbers of Irish journalists, who were nevertheless bound by its legislative – hence structural – constraints.
14 This is not to deny the fact that many people of Irish descent lost their lives in the September 11th attacks. (See The Irish Times, September 7th, 2002)

EU summit in Barcelona, where he was, conversely, seeking a summit declaration guaranteeing the protection of Irish military neutrality. (The Irish Times, March 16th, 2002). Our conclusion, therefore, is that while the discursive positions documented in this paper may be indicative of something inherently national, and culturally based, this is not to preclude them from being used, internally, to disguise profound gaps between the actuality and image of national-identity – or function, as Bourdieu puts it, as "second-order strategies aimed at disguising the first-order strategies" (Bourdieu, 1977: 43).

References

Bourdieu, Pierre. 1977. *Outline of a theory of Practice*. Cambridge: Polity Press

Burke, Kenneth. 1969. *A Grammar of Motives*. Berkley, Los Angeles, London: University of California Press (original 1945)

Chouliaraki, Lille and Fairclough, Norman. 1999. *Discourse in Late Modernity: Rethinking Critical Discourse Analysis*. Great Britain: Edinburgh University Press

Fairclough, Norman. 1995. *Media Discourse*. Great Britain: Arnold

Horgan, John. 2001: *Irish Media: A Critical History Since 1992*. London and New York.: Routledge

Jager, Siegfried. 2001. "Discourse and knowledge: Theoretical and methodological aspects of a critical discourse and dispositive analysis". In *Methods of Critical Discourse Analysis*, Ruth Wodak and Michael Meyer (eds), 34-62. London, New Delhi: Sage

Ruth Wodak. 2001: "The discourse-historical approach". In *Methods of Critical Discourse Analysis*, Ruth Wodak and Michael Meyer (eds), 63-94 London, New Delhi: Sage

Tannen, Deborah. 1993. "What's in a Frame?: Surface Evidence for Underlying Expectations" In *Framing in Discourse*, Deborah Tannen (Ed). New York, Oxford: Oxford University Press

The Guardian, Monday September 24, 2001. "Burning issues", By Roy Greenslade

The Independent, September 15th, 2001. "Terror In America: Broadcasting: Complaints Over Anti-American Comments By 'Question Time' Audience", Louise Jury Media Correspondent

The Irish Times, March 14, 2002. "Ahern brushes off Trimble's latest criticisms" By Patrick Smyth, Washington Correspondent

The Irish Times, March 16, 2002. "Ahern seeks EU pledge on neutrality before Nice vote" By Denis Staunton, Barcelona

The Irish Times, September 7, 2002 "New book recalls trauma suffered by Irish-Americans at Ground Zero" By Deaglan DE Breadan, Foreign Affairs Correspondent

Van Dijk, Teun A. (1998): "Opinions and Ideologies in the Press". In *Approaches to Media Discourse*, Allan Bell and Peter Garret (Ed), 21-64. Oxford and Massachusetts: Blackwell Publishers.

BETWEEN MEMORY AND TABOO

On the construction of images of history
in Austrian mass media discourse[1]

Alexander Pollak

My current research on the discursive construction of images of history in Austrian mass media is part of a larger interdisciplinary project called "The Making of History. Confrontation with a Taboo." The project deals with collective and individual memories on the nazi-past – and particularly on the German Wehrmacht and its role in the war of extermination – in Austria and Germany.

In my paper I focus on the role of Austrian media in two identity- and power-related projects of the post-World War II-period:

(1) the political project of constructing Austrian national identity and denying responsibility for the nazi-crimes and

(2) the public "project" of establishing an innocent perspective on World War II that allows the memorization of this event without raising and (self-)critically reflecting the question of guilt and responsibility for he nazi-crimes.

What makes Austria such an interesting site to study the use of specific constructions of the past as a means to reach certain political aims, is

---

1   This paper integrates and extends a paper written in 2000 dealing with the peculiarities of the language used and the discursive strategies applied to construct an "innocent" view on the nazi-past in Austria after 1945: Alexander Pollak, "When guilt becomes a foreign country", in: Daniel Nelson and Miriam Dedaic (eds.): *At War with Words*, The Hague: Mouton de Gruyter (in print).

the fact that even though Austria had been an integral part of the 'Third Reich', participating strongly in the Nazi-crimes, it was able to build up a positive self-image after the war, presenting itself as an innocent collective. Part of this positive self-construction was on the one hand the marginalization of the victims of the nazi-crimes and on the other hand the suppression of prevalent German-national beliefs in Austria.

I will distinguish between three mythological narratives that became the major founding myths of the Second Austrian Republic, key-narratives that had two characteristics in common: (1) they served certain political aims and (2) they were counter-factual in the sense that they ignored and contradicted historiographical knowledge. Whereas the myth of Austria as the first victim of Nazi-Germany and the myth that a completely new Austria had been born in 1945 were state-produced narratives, the claim that the German Wehrmacht had not been involved in war crimes – the so called myth of the "clean" Wehrmacht – was mainly produced by the former military elite and disseminated through literature and through the mass media and became a belief shared by large parts of the population.

My paper focuses on two questions:
- What was the role of the media in the communication of mythological narratives produced by the political elite, narratives that where related to and based on the narrative of Austria as the first victim of Nazi-Germany?
- How did Austrian mass media deal with three – partly conflicting – demands:
    (1) The demand of the political elite that the Austrian involvement in the nazi crimes should not be made a public topic but at the same time the very existence of the Nazi-crimes should not be denied.
    (2) The demand of large parts of the population that they shouldn't be burdened with guilt and responsibility for the Nazi-crimes
    (3) The war-generation's desire to talk about Second World War and communicate – on a selective basis – their war-memory.

Media-discourse

Before I am going to present the results of my research, I would like outline my approach to mass media-discourse:

I distinguish between three perspectives on mass media discourse:
(1) a *functional* perspective
(2) a perspective that focuses on the *process* of media-communication and
(3) a perspective that aims at *situating* and *classifying* individual media-representatives or groups of media-representatives within society.

(1) Concerning the functional perspective on mass media discourse, I see three major functions of mass media within society:
- *an informative function* – media function as gate-keepers, as social actors that acquire and receive, filter and process and finally transport information to the public.
- *a creative function* (constructing reality) – mass media have an autonomous role in constructing a certain reality, in producing and disseminating certain contents, and in this context in the production and reproduction of power-relations, of social structures and hierarchies.
- *a regulative function* – mass media regulate social/discursive practices, give an answer to the question how one can or should talk about events and which ones are to be talked about at all. Mass media act as moral authority that not only inform the public about the opinion of the political leaders, the political leaders about the opinion of the public and all media-consumers about the opinion of the media itself, but also communicate what I call the frame and the shape of the sayable, of the socially tolerable and reasonable (at a given point of time).

(2) The process of media communication:
Mass media do not only communicate *to* the public but also *with* a certain public, that is media communication is not a one-way but a two-way street. Media communication is always based on interaction between

the text-producer and the – potential – text-recipients. Media try to establish an identity-relationship with media-consumers. Hence, a given media text does not only mirror the view of the author about a certain topic, but displays also the assumptions of the author with respect to the text-recipients.

(3) Classifying/situating media-representatives:
In order to take into account the heterogeneity of mass media, media-representatives have to be situated within society. That is, it has to be asked, with whom the respective media-representative wants to establish an identity-relationship – with the political/economic elite, with certain parties, with certain parts of the population, with the "common people", with a "critical" public, etc. – and how are the media-functions hierarchized by certain media-representatives? Is the creative function in the first place? Or the informative function?

The classification of media-representatives according to their respective functional and procedural characteristics and modes shows the spectrum of a (more or less) heterogeneous media-landscape and of the different realities (or approaches to a common reality) that exist – or rather: are constructed – within a society. For my investigation, I had to distinguish between "statesmanlike" (mostly political dependent) and "populist" (independent) media and between media-representatives that had a critical or uncritical stance toward Austria's nazi past.

Mass media and images of history

When mass media refer to the past this takes place in the form of images of history. For the construction of certain images of history two components are of decisive importance: First, images of history consist of certain temporal, spatial and causal relationships of actors, actions and events within certain situational contexts. In other words: Historical events are represented through certain *representations of social actors* – including certain constructions of *material transitivity (Who does what to whom?)* and of *circumstance* – and through the *construction of certain causal chains* (as well as through certain temporal and spatial orderings), thereby *creating a certain perspective* and an *implicit evaluation* of the historical event. Secondly, beside the production/construction of certain historical realities, the contextualization of these historical realities within the present is of central importance in mass media discourse. Here the question is: Which are the present related issues and debates the historical events are related to?

The ideological aspects of construing certain images of history are evident. Dealing with the past and employing certain conceptions of the past is no end in itself. The past becomes of interest in contexts where it can be linked to the present. Hence, images of history serve the aim of constructing a particular present. Since individuals and groups have different – and often contradictory – perspectives on how the present (and the future) should look like, there is a permanent struggle both for the accepted/dominant perspective on the past and the valid connection of the past with the present. Images of history become powerful in that, as they are established, points of identification are being created. These serve the constitution of new, or the modification of existing identity-constructions. Summing up, specific conceptions of history are aimed at supporting and transporting specific present-day values and identity-concepts, in order to preserve or change existing views and power relations.

THE YEARS FROM 1945 TO 1955

Let us start with the immediate post-war period, the years 1945 to 1955: The political elite propagated as identity-building narratives on the one hand the victim-narrative and on the other hand the distinction between positive „Austrianess" and negative "Germaness". Both, the victim- and the Austrianess-ideology were reproduced by the media:

The reasoning behind establishing and reproducing the victim thesis as a central narrative was as simple as it was convincing: A country that had been assaulted by a hostile foreign power and had been extinguished from the political map could not be made responsible for the deeds of the assaulting power. According to this argumentation, the population of the "Ostmark" had lived under foreign law and had served in a foreign army with foreign tasks. One central image in this context is that of the Austrian soldiers[2] who were "pressed" into the German Wehrmacht and "forced" to wear "foreign" uniforms. Thus, the crimes of "the Nazis" were not "their" (the Austrians) crimes and the years from 1938 to 1945 could be presented as *"an enormous catastrophe to the Austrian people"*[3] rather than a catastrophe co-caused by many Austrians. The victim-construction had the function to externalize guilt, that is to blame the Germans for being the only ones responsible for the crimes committed.

In addition to the accounts asserting the victim-status of the Austrian people, strong emphasis – or rather, overemphasis – was given to the Austrian resistance movement, thereby trying to prove that the Austrian population had contributed a lot to the defeat of the national socialist regime and that Austria thus deserved its freedom and independence.

Inherent in the victim- as well as in the resistance-narrative was the accentuation of alleged differences between the character of Austrians and Germans. The political actors as well as the media enforced stereotypical beliefs about the "human" Austrians on the one side and the "brutal and unscrupulous" Germans. A clear line was drawn between the German "Nazis" and the Austrians.

Though the fact that that the media reproduced the main political narratives – victim-thesis, resistance-narrative, Austrianess-ideology -, media-texts showed a more contradictory picture than the one propagated by the political elite. Media-texts covered the trials against war-criminals and published accounts about national-socialist crimes. This coverage had the potential to spark discussions about the question of guilt and responsibility. But it was not the aim of the media – which were in the immediate postwar period very close to the political parties in Austria – to contradict the ideology of the political elite. Therefore the media did not only reproduce the distinction between good Austrians and evil Germans but established another distinction between the "good" Wehrmacht and the "evil" SS. The execution of the national socialist policy of extermination was solely

---

2   About 1.2 Million Austrian soldiers served in the German Wehrmacht.
3   E. F., „Tag der Befreiung", *Neues Österreich*, 13. April 1946, Seite 1.

attributed to the – relatively small group – of SS-members, whereas the Wehrmacht was presented as having fought a „regular" war and as having been unwillingly "abused" by the national socialist leadership.

THE YEARS FROM 1956 TO 1970

With the end of the allied occupation of Austria in 1955 there was a fundamental change in the general political conditions and in the conditions of the media. Whereas the political elite and the politically dependent part of the media continued using the victim narrative as a central discursive resource to suppress questions of guilt or reparations, independent media placed another narrative into the foreground, a narrative that had much more power in establishing an identity-relationship with large parts of the public. Austrian mass media chose a particular event of the war to become a symbol for the whole war: the battle of Stalingrad.

In media accounts, "Stalingrad" became a symbol for the whole war in the East and particularly a symbol for the fate of the "normal" German/Austrian soldiers. The event of "Stalingrad" served as an identity-founding construct – that is, as a point of reference for showing the cruelty of the war and as evidence supporting the collective victimization of Wehrmacht soldiers. The war was put into the literary form of a tragedy, a tragedy for the soldiers who participated, and a tragedy for the German/Austrian people as a whole.

In order to attribute to the battle of Stalingrad the functions mentioned above, it was necessary to construct a specific "Stalingrad". Suffering was reserved for the German Army. In media accounts, the *"unutterable physical and psychological suffering"*[4] of the soldiers of the Sixth Army was emphasized. That the Sixth German Army – on their long way to Stalingrad – had killed civilians and POW's and had strongly cooperated with and supported SS-units killing Jews was at that time entirely absent in Austrian media. Nevertheless, the question of guilt and responsibility was raised,

---

4   Fritz Wöss, „Stalingrad: Nicht eine Tragödie, sondern ein Verbrechen", *Neues Österreich*, 19. Jänner 1958.

but in a different way. Points of discussion were the responsibility for the military defeat in Stalingrad and the question who was to be blamed for the "crime" on the hundreds of thousands Austrian/German soldiers who had died during the battle.

Reducing the questions of guilt and responsibility to the fate of the German/Austrian soldiers and, thereby, avoiding a discussion of war crimes committed by the Sixth Army during its advance lead to the creation of an image of WW II large parts of the Austrian population and particularly the war-generation could easily identify with.

Beside the rise of the Stalingrad-narrative another discursive phenomenon started in the fifties, the "hitlerization" of the historical discourse: Media accounts started focusing on Adolf Hitler. In these accounts it seemed that nobody but him had the will to go to war, and that he was making war against the will of his people.

THE YEARS 1971 TO 1985

At the end of the sixties and the beginning of the seventies a more critical view on the past started to evolve in Austria, a critical view that called attention to existing continuities to the national socialist era and to undiscussed elements of guilt and responsibility. As a counter-reaction some parts of Austrian media – especially the "Kronenzeitung", which is famous as the newspaper read by a larger percentage of its country's population than any other newspaper in the western world – demanded to ultimately end the debate and rule off the question of guilt and responsibility – the question that had never been really dealt with.

Austrian media was at that time split into three parts:
(1) media-titles that were close to the political establishments and that still reproduced both of the two paradigmatic narratives, the victim-narrative and the Stalingrad-narrative.
(2) independent media-titles that demanded an end to any debate about guilt and responsibility and that followed the strategy of relativizing the nazi-crimes. Those media-titles rejected the victim-narrative from a german-nationalist perspective.

(3) and finally independent media-titles which took a more and more critical position to the untruthful way Austria had dealt with ist nazi-past.

Yet, during the seventies, still the uncritical approaches remained the dominant ones. Characteristical for those uncritical approaches were two discursive strategies:
- § Relativizing the nazi-past
- § Individualizing and biographizing the history of WW II and thus backgrounding the context of a war of extermination

Relativizing the past

Relativizing the past means detaching past events from their uniqueness and putting them into a context in which they are assessed according to their relation to other events. As a strategy, relativizing the past reduces the weight of certain actions or events in order to avoid dealing with them or with related questions of guilt and responsibility.

There were two meta-strategies employed by Austrian mass media-representatives to relativize the past: (1) The comparison of German/Austrian crimes with deeds of the Allies and (2) the establishing causal chains that took responsibility from Germany and German troops for triggering the war and committing crimes.

(1) Comparison with the deeds of the Allies

The comparison of German and Austrian crimes with deeds of the Allies allowed the possibility to set off one's crimes against the crimes of the former enemy while providing a chance to "normalize" German deeds by stating that they were not specific to one side only. In this context I distinguish between three media-employed relativizing strategies:
- emphasizing factual or putative war crimes of the Allies;
- presenting Allied war crimes in a far more drastic way than those committed by Germans/Austrians;

- presenting German crimes merely as a reaction to the brutal warfare of the enemy.

Emphasizing factual or putative war crimes of the allies
In many media accounts strong emphasis was given to events like the bombing of German and Austrian cities, the expulsion and persecution of the so called "Ethnic Germans" at the end and in the aftermath of the war and the massacre of Katyn. Particularly the bombing of Dresden became a symbol for Allied war-crimes. These "senseless" bombings are regarded as evidence that the Allies, too, did not shrink back from committing war crimes. At the same time the destruction of cities by the German military was marginalized in the newspaper coverage. Neither the bombing of Warsaw, Belgrade, Coventry, Stalingrad nor that of other European cities received nearly as much attention as the bombings by the Allied forces.

Other strongly accentuated issues were the expulsion and persecution of the so called "Ethnic Germans" (Volksdeutsche) in Middle and Eastern Europe at the end of and in the aftermath of the war and the massacre of Katyn, a place in Poland where thousands of Polish officers were killed by Soviet units. The latter event was given the role of an important relativizer in the media. For a period of more than forty years, the Soviet Union had denied responsibility for this crime and asserted that German units had killed Polish officers. For parts of the Austrian media Katyn provided an opportunity to state that the Soviets must come to terms with their past (rather than Austria). Moreover, by emphasizing "dark chapters" in the history of one major Ally, it was again possible to contextualize German deeds within a generally criminal period of history.

Presenting Allied war crimes in a far more drastic way than German crimes
Allied war crimes are emphasized not only by the frequency of their appearance but also by the argumentation strategies applied. Most striking about these accounts is the linguistic and semiotic manner in which they are presented. The language used and the pictures selected to describe Allied crimes and to comment on them differ significantly from the way German/Austrian crimes are presented. This leads to a potentially much

stronger and emotional perception of the Allied crimes and, again, to the backgrounding and marginalizing of German/Austrian crimes.

The language used to present crimes of the Allies is often harsh, direct and loaded with emotions. Moreover, the deeds are described in much greater detail, actors named much more often, and active constructions used with a significantly higher frequency than when describing German/Austrian crimes. The desire to emotionalize can be detected easily in cases where the naming of the actors is accompanied by amplifying/intensifying attributes, as in *"the bloodthirsty Partisans"*[5]. Or, to give a further example for the language employed: *"With their spades the Bolsheviks crushed the skulls of the wounded [German soldiers]."*[6] In contrast to these examples, "bloodlust" is never attributed to the "normal" German/Austrian soldiers. Moreover, most sentence-constructions that talk about German crimes are passive ones, like *"At that time some persons were shot."*[7] that do not mention the actor.

Presenting German crimes merely as a reaction to the brutal warfare of the enemy
A different strategy to relativize German crimes is to present them as a mere reaction to preceding crimes or brutalities of the enemy. This argumentative strategy comes fully into play when talking about – or rather, justifying – German/Austrian action against Partisans in Greece and Yugoslavia. An example of such is: *"Especially in Yugoslavia, but also in Greece, a merciless partisan warfare, several years lasting, was initiated by [the partisan leader] Josip Broz-Tito who after the war became the head of state of Yugoslavia. Actions of Tito-Partisans against the German occupants provoked their cruel reactions, ..."*[8]

---

5   Wolfgang Oberleitner, 27 March 1986, "Als der Sohn den Vater toetet", *Die Presse*.
6   Ingomar Pust, 31 January 1976, "Sowjets toeteten alle Verwundeten", *Neue Kronenzeitung*.
7   "Ich stand an der Grube und schoss", 23 October 1962, *Wiener Zeitung*.
8   Presse Lexikon, 6 March 1986, "Balkanfeldzug", *Die Presse*.

(2) Transforming the causal chain

When analyzing or explaining past events like the Second World War, media accounts tend to build up a causal chain. Starting from somewhere in the past, certain actions or events are said to have caused subsequent actions or events, thus constructing a particular explanatory path through history. Hence, one powerful way to change the perception of past events is by altering or reassessing a major link of the chain, thereby transforming the entire causal chain.[9]

The question of the responsibility for triggering war in 1939

One major causal link constructed in media accounts is the responsibility for unleashing World War II. Many German and Austrian historical revisionists have "specialized" on this topic. They see a possibility to mitigate German/Austrian guilt by either asserting that war was inescapable or emphasizing that the Allies – particularly Great Britain and the Soviet Union – were also responsible for the outbreak of the war (or at least for the war becoming a world war).

While the criticism of the so called "Westmächte" (western powers) is often presented subtly, the Soviet Union is far more openly made responsible for war's outbreak. In this context, central importance is ascribed to the Stalin-Hitler Pact (otherwise known as the Molotov-Ribbentrop Pact), i.e., a non-aggression treaty that also allotted conquered territories in Eastern Europe. Some of the accounts dealing with this accord and the outbreak of the war attribute a passive role to the Soviet Union, that is, the pact between the Soviet Union and the German Reich is seen as rear cover for Hitler's plans of conquest. Other accounts assess Stalin as holding all cards in his hand, and as culpable for the decisive impulse for the war's outbreak. In their most extreme form such assessments see Stalin as *"having abused Hitler as a ram against the capitalist democracies of the*

---

9 See Alexander Pollak, "When guilt becomes a foreign country", in: Daniel Nelson and Miriam Dedaic (eds.): *At War with Words*, The Hague: Mouton de Gruyter (in print).

West".[10] Consequently, the German attack on Poland becomes, *"in its depth"* a strategic move of the Soviet Union.[11]

Assessing the German attack on the Soviet Union in 1941

With the German attack on the Soviet Union in June 1941 an unprecedented war of extermination had begun. Millions of killed civilians and prisoners of war, and the industrial killing of millions of Jews by German units in the course of the so-called "Final Solution", were parts of the war in the east. The question of guilt and responsibility is directly connected with activities of German soldiers and members of *"Sondereinheiten"* [special units] during the war in the East. Hence, one strategy by which to deny or relativize guilt is to transfer responsibility from the perpetrator to the victim, from the attacker to the attacked. The *"Präventivkriegsthese"* [preventive war thesis][12] thus attempts to transfer responsibility for German attacks on the Soviet Union to the Soviet Union by asserting that Germans had only anticipated, and thereby prevented, an already planned Soviet attack. In such accounts, an image is drawn of the situation prior to the German attack that aims to justify and naturalize such a decision.

Biographical accounts – experiences of individuals

Beside the relativizing approach, Austrian media was also dominated by the backgrounding of the crimes and the war of extermination through the "biographization" and individualization of WW II accounts. The usage of biographical accounts has a twofold impact on the creation of images of history: On the one hand, the war is brought to a more concrete and understandable level so that readers can identify with the individuals. On the other hand, the danger arises that the overall context of actions

---

10 Ernst Topitsch, 27 September 1986, "Antifaschismus", *Die Presse*.
11 Ibid.
12 The *"Praeventivkriegsthese"* (preventive war thesis) was one of the major subjects of the German *"Historikerstreit"* (historians' debate) in the 1980s.

and events is lost and that, through the selection of the biographies, a non-comprehensive and distorted image of the past is presented.

Some of the accounts about World War II have an autobiographical and/or anecdotal character. The authors make themselves and their experiences part of their story. This self-involvement is used as a means to strengthen the truth-claim of their account since, after all, they had been there. A different function of these anecdotes is opening up of the possibility that the larger context of events can be set aside, with a focus instead on the everyday life and everyday problems of specific persons. At a time of global war and industrial death camps, the world is reduced to the micro world of persons, actions and events surrounding the author.

Many authors refer to experiences of other people to form accounts about events of the Second World War. These references appear as quotations from letters, inquiries or interviews, or as life-stories of persons using quotes to illustrate these persons' experiences. Not surprisingly, accounts about "Stalingrad" contain, by a wide margin and with the highest frequency of use, all these types of biographical references. In relation to "Stalingrad" there are field-post letters – *"letters in the face of death"*[13] – quoted, autobiographical books – *"I was eyewitness in Stalingrad"*[14] – reviewed, inquiries – *"What does Stalingrad mean to you?"*[15] – carried out, and there are accounts about survivors – *"The man who escaped through two frontiers"*[16] – supported by quotes.

Obituaries are a special form of descriptive accounts, dealing with biographies of deceased persons to whom certain relevance is ascribed. In our case, most of these obituaries deal with high generals of the Wehrmacht. What is interesting about these accounts is the stereotypical beliefs about generals, which they produce and reproduce. The generals are, in a way, taken out of the context of a war of extermination and described only from a perspective dealing with their military careers. Thus,

---

13 "Briefe im Angesicht des Todes", 24 January 1953, *Kurier.*
14 "Ich war Augenzeuge in Stalingrad", 2 February 1983, *Kurier.*
15 "Was ist Stalingrad für Sie?", 18 January 1973, *Kurier.*
16 "Der Mann, der durch zwei Fronten entkam", 18 January 1973, *Kurier.*

they are ascribed attributes like *"plucky (schneidig)"*[17] or *"tough (beinhart)"*[18] and named as *"old war-horses"*[19] or as *"desert foxes (Wuestenfuechse)"*[20]. Finally, all these generals are described as having been unlucky and as not having received the honor they would have deserved.

THE YEARS 1986 UNTIL TODAY

It was only in 1986, in the course of the Waldheim affair – which was a debate about the war- and nazi-past of the Austrian presidential candidate Kurt Waldheim – that a longer-lasting and deeper debate about the way the Austrian society had dealt with its past was unleashed. The achievements of the Waldheim debate were, on the one hand, that the thesis of Austria as the first victim of Nazi-Germany was publicly and strongly questioned, and, on the other hand, that the term *"Pflichterfüllung"* [doing one's duty] in connection with the participation of the soldiers in the Second World War was reassessed, and endowed with a more negative connotation.

In 1995, another "milestone" was set by an exhibition dealing with the crimes of the German Wehrmacht during World War II,[21] which caused a controversial debate in the mass media about the role of the Wehrmacht and the "normal" soldiers in the war of extermination. Parts of the media at that time still defended the view that the soldiers were to be seen solely as innocent and as tragic victims, while other media outlets started to reassess their position.

---

17 Hans Magenschab, 26 July 1973, "Ein Tritt für einen Duce", *Kurier*.
18 Ibid.
19 Robert Vinatzer, 3 October 1976, "Ein Antikriegsbuch über Gebirgsdivision", *Kurier*.
20 "Es hat an Glück gefehlt nicht an Wert", 25 October 1992, *Die Presse*.
21 The exhibition "Vernichtungskrieg. Verbrechen der Wehrmacht 1941-1944." („*War of extermination. Crimes of the Wehrmacht from 1941 to 1944*") was shown from 1995 to 1999 in German and Austrian cities. In 1999 the exhibition was stopped because it had been accused that some of the photos shown had the wrong caption. A commission was set up by the Hamburg Institute for Social Research to investigate the correctness of the photos and the captions. Despite the fact that the commission backed the exhibition to a great extend a new exhibition was set up which opened in November 2001 in Berlin and which is again shown in Germany and Austria.

Conclusions

Let us come back to the initial question of the role of Austrian media after 1945 in dealing with political and public wants and demands concerning the handling of Austria's national socialist past:

A short period from 1945 to 1947 in which parts of the media foregrounded the national socialst crimes – particularly in the context of the large number of trials against war-criminals – and took a more critical stance toward the involvement of the population in these crimes, was followed from 1948 on by a longer period in which the accounts introduced by the political elite where taken on unquestioned by the media. That is, Austrian media propagated the victim- as well as the Austrianess-ideology, exaggerated the role of the Austrian resistance-movement, marginalized the victims of the racist national socialist policy and backgrounded prevalent German-national beliefs. Only during the media-coverage of the Eichmann-trial the construction of the Austrian victim-collective (with the NS-victims being attributed the role of a minor part of this collective) was broken and narratives of the survivors of the death-camps about their experience of the NS-crimes put into the foreground.

However, shortly after the end of the trial the accounts of war-veterans, particularly of survivors of the battle of Stalingrad were dominant again. With the Stalingrad-narrative a continuous motive was established that was enhanced by the media to a symbol for the whole Second World War and particularly as a symbol for the fate of the normal Austrian soldier.

Furthermore, with the beginning of the sixties it came to a division of the media-landscape concerning their perspective on the past: While the politically dependent media still propagated the victim-narrative, some parts of the independent media tried to establish a more "popular" uncritical perspective on the NS-period – not least by integrating German-national perceptions of the past. However, at the end of the sixties first rudiments of a critical counter-discourse emerged in some parts of the media, criticizing especially personal continuities to the NS-period, for example in the area of jurisdiction but also in political representations. With the increasing heterogeneization of the Austrian media-landscape in the seventies and eighties the representatives of a critical view on the past gained more public weight – a development that led to the intensive and very controversial debates about Austria's national socialist past from the mid of the eighties on.

I would like to highlight two – in my view – remarkable results of my investigation:

First, in the years after 1945 there was information in the media about Austrian involvement in the nazi-crimes. Yet, what was missing, was the integration of this information into coherent narratives about the years from 1938 to 1945 – rather this information remained fragmented and thus backgrounded. The dominant war-narratives, like for example the ones on the battle of Stalingrad, did not contain any remarks about the involvement of the soldiers in the war of extermination and about the systematic crimes against civilians – particularly jewish civilians – and POWs during the war.

Secondly, the critical perspective that evolved in the seventies and eighties was not created by a new generation of politicians but by a new generation of journalists and historians who called attention to the Austrian involvement in the nazi-crimes and to the untenability of the victim-narrative. Today, the victim-narrative is out of use in Austrian media while it is still used as a discursive resource by Austrian politicians.

References

Assmann, Jan. 1999. Das kulturelle Gedächtnis. Beck: München.

Bettelheim, Peter; Streibl, Robert (Hg.), 1994, Tabu und Geschichte. Wien: Picus Verlag.

Chouliaraki, Lili; Fairclough, Norman. 1999. Discourse in Late Modernity: Rethinking Critical Discourse Analysis. Edinburgh University Press, Edinburgh.

Carmen Rosa Caldas-Coulthard and Malcolm Coulthard (ed.). 1995. Texts and Practices. New York, Routledge.

Fairclough, Norman, "Discourse and text: linguistic and intertextual analysis within discourse analysis", In: Discourse & Society 3, 1992, S. 193-219.

Fairclough, Norman. 1995. Media Discourse. Arnold, London, New York.

Fowler, Roger. 1991. Language in the News. Discourse and Ideology in the Press. Routledge, London, New York.

Halbwachs, Maurice. 1991. Das kollektive Gedächtnis. Fischer Taschenbuch Verlag, Frankfurt am Main.

Halliday, M.A.K. 1994. An Introduction to Functional Grammar. Arnold, London, Melbourne, Auckland.

Hamburger Institut für Sozialforschung (Hg.), 1999, „Vernichtungskrieg. Verbrechen der Wehrmacht 1941 bis 1944", Hamburg: Hamburger Edition.

Kumpfmüller, Michael, 1995, Die Schlacht von Stalingrad. München: Fink.

Manoschek, Walter, 1995, „Serbien ist judenfrei". München: Oldenburg.

Nelson, Daniel; Dedaic, Miriam, "At War with Words", Routledge, London (in print).

Pätzold, Kurt, 2000, „Ihr wart die besten Soldaten". Ursprünge und Geschichte einer Legende. Leipzig: Militzke Verlag.

Reisigl, Martin; Wodak Ruth. 200. Discourse and Discrimination. Routledge, London

Ueberschär, Gerd R. and Wolfram Wette (ed.), 1999, Der deutsche Überfall auf die Sowjetunion, Frankfurt: Fischer Taschenbuch-Verlag.

Uhl, Heidemarie, 1992, „Zwischen Versöhnung und Verstörung", Wien: Böhlau.

Van Dijk, Teun (ed.) 1985. Handbook of Discourse Analysis. Volume 1, Academic Press, London.

Wassermann, Heinz P., 2000. „Zuviel Vergangenheit tut nicht gut!" Nationalsozialismus im Spiegel der Tagespresse der Zweiten Republik. Studien-Verlag, Innsbruck-Wien-München.

Wodak, Ruth; Menz, Florian; Mitten, Richard; Stern, Frank. 1994. Die Sprachen der Vergangenheiten. Suhrkamp, Frankfurt.

Wodak, Ruth; Pelikan, Johanna; Nowak, Peter; Gruber, Helmut; De Cilia, Rudolf; Mitten, Richard. 1990. „Wie sind alle unschuldige Täter" – Diskurshistorische Studien zum Nachkriegsantisemitismus. Suhrkamp, Frankfurt.

Ziegler, Meinrad; Kannonier-Finster, Waltraud, 1993, Österreichisches Gedächtnis. Wien: Böhlau.

IDENTITY DISCOURSE AND THE CONSTRUCTION OF IMAGES
The Role of *Le Soir* in the Belgian Identity Debate

Inge Degn

INTRODUCTION

The aim of this paper is to study certain lines of fracture and conflict in the Belgian identity debate. The study consists of an analysis of six articles from the influential Belgian Francophone daily *Le Soir*. The articles, which appeared between 1998 and 2001, deal with cultural events, primarily the publication of books etc. discussing the identity of the Belgians. The study is supplemented by an analysis of the use of the term *belgitude*, which has occupied a central place in the identity debate since 1976. The Internet archives of *Le Soir* was the source of the study as a whole.[1]

A first classification of the six articles was based on the perceived affinity of the journalist with his subject. This resulted in two groups of articles, the first of which consists of three articles presenting a conception of 'Belgian identity' which is not queried by the journalist, while the other group consists of articles that, judging from their treatment of the subject, deal with contentious issues.

The first group comprises three articles; (1) a review of a book published in 1998, *La Belgique toujours grande et belle?*, (2) an interview on the occasion of the republication in 1999 of Jacques Sojcher's *Le Professeur de*

---

1   Quotations are reproduced as they appear in this electronic version, although the layout and typography clearly differ from the printed version.

philosophie, and (3) a review of an issue of the journal *Marginales*, dedicated to a discussion of the future of Belgium. The second group consists of (4) an article dealing with the publication of an anthology on Walloon identity (*Oser être wallon!*), which appeared in 1998, (5) a report from a forum on cultural politics, at which this book, according to *Le Soir*, played an important role, and, finally, (6) a comment on a party given in honour of an Oscar-nominated Belgian film. This study examines how *Le Soir* speaks of these events as elements in an identity debate; whether a construction of identities and images is taking place, and if so, what the identities and images constructed by *Le Soir* are.

In fact, part of the answer is given already by the preliminary categorization of the articles into the two groups. The basis of this categorization is mainly the way in which the books and events in question are presented on the level of enunciation. The three articles in the first group came about as a result of *Le Soir* calling on the author or editor to comment on their publication, whereas the anthology dealt with in articles (4) and (5) is not submitted to a review proper (neither is the publication the occasion of an interview or conversation). Rather, the journalist quotes and evaluates the editor and coauthor's statements. The journalist thus places himself in a position with a privileged opportunity of categorizing some speech acts as scholarly, and others as political, and of deciding whether an issue should be subjected to debate, and whether it is acceptable and legitimate as an issue of discussion.

The present analysis draws mainly on concepts from discourse theory[2], but also applies elements of linguistic analysis to show how the individual texts function, i.e. to study the articulatory practice of specific texts on the linguistic as well as on the ideological level. According to Laclau and Mouffe, "the specificity of the hegemonic articulatory practice is given by its confrontation with other articulatory practices of an antagonistic character".[3] My hypothesis is that the discourse in *Le Soir* is a hegemonic

---

2 Cf. Ernesto Laclau and Chantal Mouffe, 1985, *Hegemony and Socialist Strategy. Towards a radical Democratic Politics*, London, Verso; Ernesto Laclau, 1996, *Emancipation(s)*, London, Verso; Ernesto Laclau, 2000, *La Guerre des identités. Grammaire de l'émancipation*, Paris, La Découverte; Jacob Torfing, 1999, *New Theories of Discourse. Laclau, Mouffe and Žižek*, Oxford, Blackwell Publishers.
3 Laclau and Mouffe, 1985, 114.

discourse that is challenged by other discourses, which it seeks to marginalize and repress in order to maintain its hegemony. The question, however, is what constitutes the identity constructed by this hegemonic discourse – the key terms *identity* and *Belgian identity* being undeniably *floating signifiers* whose meanings must be fixed by chains of equivalence and intertextual references. One of the possible interpretations is *la belgitude*, a term often encountered in Belgian debate, but one that is in itself a floating signifier. Therefore a survey has been included of the use of the term *belgitude* in *Le Soir* and of the function of that term with regard to the identity discourse.

Belgium and "Belgian Identity"

(1) Review entitled "Belgium for ever grand and beautiful (?)"[4]

The review of an anthology on Belgian identity, *Belgique toujours grande et belle*[5], appeared in the *Opinions et débats* section of *Le Soir* (20 October 1998). The headline is eponymous with the title of the book, which in its own turn references the Belgian national anthem, *la Brabançonne*, but with the question mark appended. The presentation of the book gives another intertextual reference; the article refers in fact to a 1980 issue of the *Revue de l'Université de Bruxelles, la belgique malgré tout*[6], dedicated to the topic of Belgium. The words used to present the book are clearly positive: "It's a resurrection – it's amusing, surprising, and vivifying,"[7] and the subject of the book is said to be "'Belgian identity', for better or for worse" (article's inverted commas)[8]. This stands in contrast to the just mentioned earlier issue of the journal which described a non-identity.[9] The new book is seen

---

4 *"Belgique toujours grande et belle(?)"*
5 *Belgique toujours grande et belle* (edited by Jacques Sojcher and Antoine Pickels), Bruxelles, *Revue de l'Université de Bruxelles*, 1998.
6 The article says that this book, *la belgique malgré tout*, published in 1980 and edited by Jacques Sojcher is "le grand classique sur le sujet" (the Belgian question) and declares that the concept of *belgitude* was created in this book. This is not the case. The word *belgitude* was created by the sociologist Claude Javeau on the model of *negritude* and appeared for the first time in 1976 in a special issue of the *Nouvelles littéraires* edited by Pierre Mertens with the title "L'Autre Belgique".
7 *C'est une résurrection. Drôle, imprévue, stimulante.*
8 *bon gré mal gré, «l'identité belge».*
9 *un sentiment «en creux», donnait une non-définition.*

105

simply as corresponding to the reality of the country: 126 public figures present their perception of their country, a society best characterised as a mosaic,[10] but with a pervading feature of irony, humour – a certain distance,[11] something which the journalist discerns as well in the title of the book, which is understood to be ironical. In other words, to speak of Belgium and Belgian identity appears to necessitate a *manoeuvre*; one has to speak of them in a circumlocutory way, as it were. Among the positive features is also counted the fact that the book contains several Flemish contributions considered as "analyses that clearly dissociate themselves from the visions of the future identified with Van den Brande and Peeters".[12] They are presented as politicians demanding further Flemish autonomy, with a partition of Belgium as a possible result. The fact that none of the contributors are politicians is also seen as a positive trait, as they would only have had inadequate solutions with little bearing on the realities of the country.[13] The reader is led into answering the question of the title affirmatively, although the text does not specify what is to be understood by 'the reality of the country' (*la réalité du pays*), or by 'Belgian identity' (*l'identité belge*). However, the text draws a line negating and excluding Flemish nationalism and political adjustments of the Constitution and its institutions. The review itself is followed by five excerpts from the book, confirming the impression of a 'mosaic', rather than fixing the meaning of these terms. The paragraph introducing the excerpts from the book repeats the already mentioned characteristics with a slightly different, but still exclusively positive wording: "In the present work, 'la belgitude' is replaced by a motley, multifaceted, critical view."[14]

The first excerpt is authored by Jacques Sojcher, a co-editor of the book as well as of *la belgique malgré tout*. This professor of philosophy at the Free University of Brussels (Université libre de Bruxelles) is also the interviewee of the following text.

---

10 *société civile aux allures de mosaïque.*
11 *la prise de distance, l'humour, l'ironie.*
12 *analyses, qui prennent clairement leurs distances avec les versions Van den Brande ou Peeters de l'avenir.*
13 *des modèles inadéquats, peu conformes à la réalité du pays.*
14 *La «belgitude» a laissé la place dans cet ouvrage à une vision bigarrée, multiple, critique.*

(2) Interview with Jacques Sojcher, philosopher "You must come from somewhere in order to appreciate the world"[15]

This article (*Le Soir*, 17 March 1999, no indication of section) is an interview on the occasion of the republication of Jacques Sojcher's book *Le professeur de philosophie*,[16] which is characterized as a plea for the preservation of a vital and multiple Belgian culture and identity.[17] The journalist's initial reference to *La Belgique toujours grande et belle* offers an opportunity to repeat the evaluation of the book, quoted in (1): The image of a multifaceted country characterized by uncertain feelings of belonging,[18] which in the context should be interpreted positively. In the interview, a dichotomy is created between "the multiplication of identities" and "a hermetically fixed identity"[19]. The latter collocation signals a clear, almost automatic dissociation from any claim to a national identity (i.e. understood as different from a Belgian identity). This also explains why a vague belonging can be positive, as it cannot be self-contained (*repli*) and strained (*crispé*). The other pole of the dichotomy, on the contrary, is displayed through a long description maintaining that a sense of belonging still exists as a force that unifies "the multiple identities" (*ces identités multiples*). "Although the sense of belonging is frail, it does exist".[20] Jacques Sojcher's exposition does preserve a theoretical dialectics between the right to be different and the universal; however the examples that he gives from the Belgian context serve to construct a polarity between the *we*-group united by its belonging to Belgium and an impersonal *one*. To this *one* is attributed a range of nationalist positions, e.g. the desire to force on the *we* either a union with France (with its grandeur and national pride), or "a nationalism a la Van den Brande", or an "oversensitive and over excluding nationalism"[21] which is said to germinate in the Walloons. The picture of the nationalist Flanders is but suggested, whereas the picture of Wallonia appears

---

15 "*Il faut être de quelque part pour apprécier le monde.*"
16 Jacques Sojcher, *Le Professeur de philosophie*, Bruxelles, Labor, 1999, first published in 1976.
17 *livre-plaidoyer pour une culture vivante et l'identité plurielle.*
18 *l'image d'un pays mosaïque au sentiment d'appartenance diffus…*
19 *la multiplication des identities; le repli identitaire crispé.*
20 *Même ténu, le sentiment d'appartenance existe; une appartenance commune.*
21 *un nationalisme frileux promulgant l'exclusion* presents yet another example of the ubiquitous collocations.

more clear-cut. Sojcher mentions the large companies of the past (making them explicitly Walloon!) now in French possession (*la Générale, Cockerill, Petrofina*...), the debts, and the much-criticized Walloon national anthem (*la dette de la Wallonie, hymne ringard, hymne idiot*). What he is exerting here is a sort of collective bullying by means of doubtful stereotypes. In contrast to these images, he paints a picture of the Belgian 'specificity': "a way of life, a way of meeting, of compromizing... It's a climate, a geography, a history – in short a common culture, attached not only to the language or to the region, although the two societies become more and more estranged to each other.... There's a predeliction for the bad taste, a way of making oneself at home... Basically, Belgium is an opaque experience".[22] Apart from the almost obligatory self-abasement, one notes the vague but verbose descriptions that can be seen as a sort of overlexicalisation. The intention seems to be one of fixing the meaning of the signifier *la spécificité belge* by metaphors, but apart from "living and meeting" (this must be a tautology as a society can hardly be imagined without it) and "feeling good at home" (likewise), he defines it solely in negative terms: Despite the fact that the country is divided, and the two communities are having still less to do with each other, thus becoming increasingly estranged from each other, the author insists on a different reality – the existence of" a common culture that does *not* depend exclusively on language or region."[23] But what is not made explicit by Sojcher. He concludes by suggesting a union on a different level, a "crossbreed" with the (unspecified) other(s),[24] a union that would transcend the old identity and the ethnic identities. This appears to be an individualist solution to the *de facto* division of the country that was just pointed out.

It should be noted that no explicit examples of the claimed multiculturalism are given whereas the traditional ethnic groups or populations of Belgium are indeed mentioned. The effort here is directed towards a

---

22 *un art de vivre, une façon de se rencontrer, de bricoler des compromis... Il y a un climat, une géographie, une histoire, une culture commune pas uniquement liée à la langue ou à la région, même si les deux communautés se connaissent de moins en moins... Il y a un goût du mauvais goût, une façon d'être bien chez soi... La Belgique, au fond, est une évidence opaque.*
23 *une culture commune pas uniquement liée à la langue ou à la region.*
24 *"un métissage, ce 'devenir autre' en restant soi-même."*

construction of Belgium as a field of identification, in other words, there is an attempt to arrest the flow of differences.

(3) Review of Marginales: "La Belgique: stop ou encore?"
The last example of this type of identity article that we will have a look into is a review of an issue of the periodical *Marginales* (no. 234) entitled *La Belgique: stop ou encore?* (*Le Soir*, 25 June 1999). The review was carried in the section *Opinions et débats*. As was the case with the interview above (2), this text is likewise preoccupied with the question of how a dissolution of Belgian unity can be checked. The editor explains the title's question, which was presented to 24 Belgian writers (*"24 écrivains encore toujours belges"*). In his view, the choice before the Belgians is between two alternatives, one involving making an effort and showing tolerance, the other being laziness and a lack of tolerance: "[we should] reflect on what this *utopia* in the heart of Europe has been able to accomplish with regard to *tolerance in the administration of complexity*, [and we should likewise reflect on] whether it is really responsible to destroy so much *effort* in the pursuit of an autonomy which often reflects no more than a *laziness* of the heart and spirit" (my italics).[25] Judging from *Le Soir*'s article the answers returned demonstrate emotion rather than analysis. They refer to "the existence of a Belgium that is "multifarious, motley and mixed"[26] and to the threat, with which some of them seem obsessed, that the country may split up and disappear irrevocably: "the nightmare vision of the country's dissolution, its disruption and disappearance" as well as "a number of apocalyptic visions".[27] One should not be surprised, then, that the plea for an *encore* prevails. This answer is pronounced by a *we* as it can be seen in the article's concluding answer which is a quotation of the last line in Ionesco's (absurdist) drama *La leçon*: *Continuons! continuons!*

An undivided Belgium is obviously the frame of reference of the preceding texts, which construct a positive picture of Belgian identity

---

25 *se demander ce que cette* utopie *au cœur de l'Europe a pu réaliser sur le plan de la* gestion tolérante de la complexité, *et s'il est vraiment sérieux de liquider tant d*'efforts *dans une course à l'autonomie qui n'est souvent que l'expression d'une* paresse *du cœur et de l'esprit* (my italics).
26 *l'existence d'une Belgique, plurielle, bigarrée, métissée.*
27 *spectre de la décomposition, de la dislocation et de la disparition du pays; plusieurs visions d'apocalypse.*

that may be summarized under the heading of the above-mentioned "tolerance in the administration of complexity".[28] In this imagery, other identities emerge on the frontiers of the identity landscape; the tolerance, openness and inclusion of the authors meet with attitudes characterized by nationalism, rejection and exclusion, attributed to the others in their construction of competing Walloon and Flemish identities. This line of conflict is manifest in the articles that we shall analyse in the following sections.

LINES OF CONFLICT
A Walloon Identity?

(4) Van Cauwenberghe campaigning against 'elite' culture. Cut down on contemporary dance and increase spending on Walloon theatre, says Charleroian minister..[29]
Appearing in the section *Actualité politique et sociale* of *Le Soir*, 28 August 1998, this article is the closest one gets to a review of *Oser être wallon!*[30], an anthology edited by Van Cauwenberghe, or Van Cau, then a minister in both the Walloon government and in the government of the French Community. The headline of the article reproduces some of the Charleroian Van Cauwenberghe's statements at the publication of the book. Only a further perusal of the article makes its reader realize that it is actually a treatment of the book. Its title is reproduced and the cover described (yellow and red, decorated with the bold cock, *le coq hardi*, emblem of the Walloon Region). The ensuing paragraph names the subjects and the authors of six out of fourteen contributions. This is seasoned with a quotation from an article. The reader is thus led to believe that this is a book on Walloon identity.

However, in using the word *pretends* the journalist indicates his view that the book is *not* a contribution to the debate on Walloon identity,[31]

---

28   *la gestion tolérante de la complexité.*
29   *Van Cauwenberghe en campagne contre la culture 'élitiste'. Moins pour la danse contemporaine et plus pour le théâtre wallon, plaide le ministre carolo..*
30   *Oser être wallon ! Ouvrage collectif à l'initiative de Jean-Claude Van Cauwenberghe*, Gerpinnes, Quorum, 1998.
31   *Van Cauwenberghe prétend vouloir simplement apporter une contribution au débat sur l'identité wallonne.*

but rather a political manifestation, *un geste politique*. The journalist's position may explain his choice of what seems to be a mixing of genres in the article: reporting an event (the dominant genre); review (the second paragraph); and political comment, as indicated by its placement in the section *Actualité politique et sociale*. The reporting (from the presentation of the book) deals primarily with Van Cauwenberghe's speech, which is the only one mentioned, but also takes up Van Cauwenberghe's contribution to the book. It is categorized as not belonging to an intellectual debate, but rather to a political debate. A warning is given against the position imputed to Van Cauwenberghe, not least its long-term consequences; namely a regionalization of culture, education and broadcasting. Both the title and the text as such operate with a division of culture into elite culture (*danse contemporaine, institutions culturelles de prestige, Charleroi-Danse*) vs. Walloon dialectal theatre (*théâtre dialectal*). The responsibility for this division is attributed to Van Cauwenberghe, who is said to give priority to the Walloon dialectal theatre. The chains of equivalences established by this manoeuvre fix the meaning of the signifiers *la Wallonie* and *la Communauté française*.

The journalist cleverly avoids using the same model when dealing with the other contributions. Otherwise he might have come into conflict with the deduced dichotomy (the authors as a whole defining themselves as Walloons and thus fundamentally positive to the Walloon culture) or he might have marginalized the body of Walloon intellectuals and cultural figures contributing to the book. On the contrary, this risk is warded off by making another division of authors and articles, viz. by classifying them as belonging to either *science* or *politics*. The journalist thus operates a separating of the *intellectual* debate from the *political* debate, a categorisation which isolates Van Cauwenberghe with his aim for an ambitious identity policy from intellectuals and scientists, thus making him a target of rejection. This strategy is further reinforced by the predominance of agent-action in the second part of the article, with the effect of stressing Van Cauwenberghe's responsibility.

The second part of the "review article" carries the title of Van Cauwenberghe's contribution to the book, *L'identité fait la force*, and it deals partly with Van Cauwenberghe's statements at the presentation, partly with his contribution, whose title refers to the motto of the Belgian nation-state: *L'union fait la force*. In his resumé of Van Cauwenberghe's reflections in the final chapter of the book, the journalist succeeds in attributing to him a long list of attacks, complaints, and damaging or even absurd claims: He says, he writes, he rises to resistance, he accuses (the French Community), he cites, he speculates, he asks aloud (making a sweeping claim, see below), he makes serious complaints (on education, because it denies the history of Wallonia), he advocates (more regional radio and TV), and finally, he demands, in unclear terms, at least so far (that culture, education and broadcasting be regionalized). [32] These examples show that Van Cauwenberghe is positive towards regions, instances of collective identification, the 'Walloon soul', an ambitious identity policy, and negative towards moralizers (who are warning you that identity is tantamount to nationalism) and to the French Community, which he accuses of constituting an obstacle to the development of Wallonia (*un handicap au développement de la Wallonie*).

The journalist's attitude stands out clearly in qualifications such as: "he [Van Cau] cites as a glaring example" and "he makes the sweeping claim".[33] Such expressions also serve to expose a certain populism in Van Cauwenberghe's statements. It should be noticed, however, that no claim for a regionalization of culture etc. is expressed by Van Cauwenberghe, but that this is attributed to him by the journalist.

In addition to this categorization of the publication of the book as a political act, *un geste politique*, and of Van Cauwenberghe as a political adversary, the journalist overtly holds him up to ridicule by describing how he ostensibly rode into the election campaign: "Riding astride his rooster, the Minister of the Walloon Region and of the French Community

---

32 *il dit, il écrit, il s'insurge, il accuse, il cite, il s'interroge, il se demande tout haut, il exprime de sérieuses doléances (l'histoire de la Wallonie est niée), il préconise (une accentuation dans le sens régional des programmes de la RTBF) il ne réclame pas clairement, du moins pas encore (la régionalisation de la culture, de l'enseignement et de l'audiovisuel).*

33 *il (Van Cau) cite comme exemple criant; il se demande tout haut.*

enters the election campaign."[34] Dissociation from Walloon identity is also demonstrated by his choice of words: *cette fameuse identité wallonne*. It is also striking how the quotation chosen to exemplify the scientific contributions is one that makes the identity annul itself: "The Wallonians are fortunate to have a strong identity; but also have the bad luck of being unaware of this[35] (quoted from Yves de Wasseige, an economist and formerly a member of the parliament). However, the most striking textual feature is its hierarchy of enunciation; while Van Cauwenberghe's utterances are always mediated by narration or quotation, the journalist exerts his power through his authoritative categorisations of the book and its contributions, but as well through his choices of genre, topics and quotations. This boundary between the levels of enunciation points out a political antagonism.

The article merely suggests another line of fracture in its final lines when it reproduces Van Cauwenberghe's statement that it is up to the Socialist Party to discuss a further regionalisation. The Socialist Party is Francophone, i.e. it comprises Walloon Socialists as well as Socialists in Brussels. The organization of the party, which corresponds to the institutional organization (the French Community), would seem to be conflicting with Walloon identity (the latter corresponding to another institutional level, the Region). One might then expect a possible conflict between the two levels of political identity, as represented by the party affiliation and the "regional" identity.

This fault line appears decidedly clearer in the following text, which also deals with the relationship between Wallonia and Brussels, yet without any explicit reference to the French Community.

---

34 *le ministre wallon et communautaire a enfourché le fier gallinacé pour filer vers les elections.*
35 *Les Wallons ont la chance d'avoir une forte identité et la malchance de ne pas s'en rendre compte.*

(5) A regional gumboil in Picqué's mouth: "Should we regionalize the cultural sector?" The controversy occupied the minds at the Socialist Party cultural forum this weekend ..[36]

Following only a few days after the article treated above, another article referring explicitly to Van Cauwenberghe's book and his alleged threat to regionalize the cultural sector was published (*Le Soir*, 31 August 1998). It reports from a forum on cultural politics held by the Socialist Party during the weekend of August 28-29, 1998. After the article, large extracts of a speech given by the Minister of Cultural Affairs of the French Community, Charles Picqué, are reproduced (cf. the extract below). The article, with the same byline as text (4), carries the headline: "A regional gumboil in Picqué's mouth", while the subhead asks: "Should we regionalize the cultural sector?", and informs the reader of the occasion of the speech: The controversy occupied the minds at the Socialist Party cultural forum this weekend.

Having thus set out the circumstances, the article arrives at the crux of the story, viz. Picqué's wording of a statement, which is perceived as scandalous. The ostensible affair is this sentence: "Dear comrades, I would be happy to talk about culture all day, but it feels like there's a gumboil in my mouth"[37], a formulation that sets off an avalanche of somatic or pathological phrases concerning the oral cavity, illness and taboo: "be on everybody's lips", "choking on it'", "the affected oral region", "spitting it out", "puncturing the abscess", "a minor complaint".[38] The first paragraph of the article as a whole thus displays a metaphor for toothache and impediment of speech.

The second paragraph returns to the main question of a possible regionalization of the cultural sector, referring explicitly to the anthology *Oser être wallon!* Caution is demonstrated with this issue: there is a predominance of nominalizations, of reflexive and passive constructions without agent or of constructions with an unidentified agent, the *on*. The following is

---

36 *Une carie régionaliste dans la bouche de Picqué Régionaliser la culture ? La controverse occupait les esprits au forum culturel du PS ce week-end…*

37 *Chers camarades, je veux bien parler toute la journée de la culture, mais j'ai comme une carie dans la bouche.*

38 *sur toutes les lèvres, avoir en travers de la gorge, la région stomatologique affectée, il fallait que cela sorte, crever l'abcès, la petite gene.*

the sole example of a clear, personal agent: "Van Cauwenberghe having spiced his statements (...)"[39] Another noticeable feature is the fact that the journalist persistently refers to the Wallonian regionalists as *certains, au Sud* (intimating that they number no more than a few people) and as *l'intérêt sudiste*. This renaming is strongly rejected by those who, like Van Cauwenberghe, insist on the designations *Walloon* and *Wallonia*.

The vocabulary of the article is colloquial or even hearty. In the third paragraph the Van Cauwenberghe anthology is spoken of as *le bouquin* (argot for *book)*, later the term *les portugaises (ses portugaises ont dû siffler)*, a colloquialism for ears, is used, hinting at the fact that Van Cauwenberghe was visiting Portugal at the time. Also Van Cauwenberghe's critique of the French Community triggers a play on words: the statements with which he seasoned *(pimenté)* the presentation are characterized as *piquants*, thus making a *double entendre* as Picqué seems to have been piqued by them.

These textual features concur to give an impression of a jovial-ironical tone, keeping a certain distance to both the Socialist Party *(camarades; remue-méninges*, which might be rendered as 'a mental removal') and to the Walloons/Van Cauwenberghe by indicating that it should be left to them to sort out their own affairs. However, the Extract carried immediately after the report contradicts this interpretation.

Extract: "Will we have anything left in common?"[40]
Excerpts from the speech held by the Cultural Minister of the French Community, Charles Picqué, at the Socialist Party Cultural Forum at La Reid on Saturday.
In the article proper, the *Extract* is referred to as a noted contribution: *une intervention remarquée*. The subhead indicates the frame of the contribution and the speaker's function, the designation *morceaux choisis* indicating that only extracts of the speech are given. This phrase might not be quite neutral, however, "morceaux choisis" designating a genre which was popular in earlier times as a pedagogical rendition of 'the thoughts of great minds'; one might see here a link to the moralizer that Van

---
39 *"Van Cau" avait pimenté ses propos(...).*
40 *«Partagerons-nous encore quelque chose?» Voici quelques morceaux choisis du discours de Charles Picqué, ministre de la culture de la Communauté française, prononcé, samedi, au Forum culturel du PS, à La Reid.*

Cauwenberghe (cf. article (4)) refused to take account of. By directly reproducing the speech without comment, the journalist hands over the word to the Minister of Cultural Affairs to a greater extent than was the case with Van Cauwenberghe. It is still the journalist, though, that has chosen the passages to be reproduced, and the organization of the text is thus still the responsibility of the journalist. The omission of comments, introductory clauses and coloration shows that the journalist does not attach importance to keeping his distance from what is said, nor to hold it up to ridicule, as with the Van Cauwenberghe text.

Picqué's contribution presents itself as a speech or even a lecture on cultural identity. As a starting point, the text proposes a dichotomy between two different forms of identity; one is seen as "an imposed, unchangeable and permanent construction".[41] This is opposed to "cultural identity". This term is seemingly neutral but, due to the opposition, it must be supposed to be 'natural', in the sense of unimposed, unconstructed and flexible. The meaning of 'cultural identity' is further determined in a succession of sentences where ' identity' is made the subject of a number of verbs, some of which are constative while others imply obligation (concerning conscience, confidence, and openness). The dichotomy of the two concepts or forms can be deduced from the predications: in contrast to the fixed identities (*identités figées*), notions of complexity, multiplicity, future as well as heritage (*complexité, multiplicité, héritage, futur*) are suggested. This part presents itself as a number of prescriptions indicating *the* legitimate way to deal with cultural identity while disapproval is expressed of 'wrong ways' of dealing with identity, e.g. as in: "fixed, immutable identities, which have been decreed once and for all, often serve ambiguous ends".[42] This almost amounts to a collocation, stigmatising *le nationalisme exclusif* and *le repli identitaire*. From the outset the text thus dichotomises commendable as well as deplorable ways of dealing with 'cultural identity' and this is observable throughout of the remainder of the text. The warning is elaborated on by an enumeration of unacceptable or dangerous attitudes

---

41 *les identités décrétées une fois pour toutes, figées dans une construction immuable.*
42 *les identités décrétées une fois pour toutes, figées dans une construction immuable servent souvent des objectifs ambigus.*

and acts such as "the instrumentalization of culture, its subordination to economics, the exaggeration of its adversarial role, the exaggeration or even sanctification of the identificatory processes, the exclusion and denial of the other."[43]

While the section carrying the cautions is characterized by deletion of the agent (nominalization) or by unclear agency (*on*), Picqué introduces in the succeeding section the *we* (*nous*) that must assume the task of developing a well-balanced identity, taking heed of both the heritage and the future, as well as of the local attachment and the universal dimension. By the first occurrence of *we/nous*, no clear definition is offered, but the next one is followed by the apposition *Wallons et Bruxellois*. The fact that those who deal with cultural identity in a criticizable or inappropriate way are not clearly identified is explained by this passage. Any direct reference to such persons is meticulously avoided for the reason that the Walloons, or as many of them as possible, should be brought to identify with this *we/nous*. The text concludes on the crucial argument that is also brought out in the headline: its potential drawback would be that there is nothing left to share any more ("Will we have anything left in common?"). The argumentation has three stages. The first consequence will be that "we will be swept away by the centrifugal forces of our economic logic"[44] indicating that those forces as well as the economic logic are intrinsically negative. The second consequence would be: "We shall witness a majority's emancipation from a minority"[45], a phenomenon characterized as odd, *étrange*, and clearly unacceptable. The *they/on* used here designates the adversaries, those who want to regionalize the cultural sector. These predictions lead to the essential argument: "The divided cannot be on the offensive."[46] The third consequence: We would lose our capability of being offensive. That is why Walloons and Brusselers should construct their destinies together.

Picqué's argumentation can be summarized as follows: We should stay united in order to retain our ability to be offensive. For what reasons and

---

43 *l'instrumentalisation de la culture, la subordination à des injonctions économiques, l'exagération du rôle contestataire, l'exagération voire la sacralisation des processus identificatoires, l'exclusion et la négation de l'autre.*
44 *Nous serons entraînés par les forces centrifuges de nos logiques économiques.*
45 *on verrait une majorité s'émanciper d'une minorité.*
46 *Ce n'est jamais dans la division qu'on est offensif.*

against whom, it is not said. But his statements are an implied answer to Van Cauwenberghe's slogan, *L'identité fait la force*. This contradiction is offered by the Belgian motto, *L'union fait la force*, which in this context is quoted with reference to *Wallonie+Bruxelles*, and with the aim of opposing (or even of oppressing) the nationalist Flemish claims for further autonomy. This unificatory act might target not only the *Communauté Wallonie+Bruxelles*, but also the union, to which the motto does actually refer, i.e. the unitary Belgium.

Thus, according to Charles Picqué, the parties of the 'identity situation' are constituted by the Flemings, the Brusselers (he does not specify the Francophone Brusselers), and the Walloons – with the Flemings identified as the enemy. The text constructs a solidarity, as in e.g. *Nous, Wallons et Bruxellois*, and it articulates an antagonism between *nous* (or part of *nous*) and *on*, the latter seeking to destroy the solidarity by separating the majority, *les Wallons*, from a minority, *les Bruxellois*. This polarity seems to correspond to another polarity, i.e. *identité culturelle vs. lien social*, as the cultural identity, which is damaging to the social ties, might develop into something pathological (*pathologie, symptômes*).

In other words, the text constructs two enemies, an interior one and an exterior one. The latter is used to motivate action against the former, i.e. those who want to regionalize the culture (and who are exclusively spoken of as *on*, meaning certain Walloons, Van Cauwenberghe et al.); as members of the same party they can be seen more as adversaries, and in the context of the national identity, they are reduced by the inclusive *nous*, comprising Walloons as well as Brusselers, and, it should be noted, designated as such, not as Francophones, a term that might bring to mind the institutional issue too forcefully.

Cultural identity is a crucial notion to the text, but it remains completely abstract. Its meaning is filled in by a chain of notions no less abstract and imprecise: 'heritage', 'future', 'local attachment' and 'openness to the universal'. The fact that no reference is given to Belgium or to the French Community (except in the paratext) could be explained by the fact that it addresses a readership that is aware of the frame of reference, but more likely it is part of a strategy of purposeful vagueness in referencing. In comparison, references to Walloon identity are unambiguous, as was the rejection of this identity in the preceding text (4) on *Oser être wallon!*

If in the preceding text we had to deduce the enemy that Picqué only implies, but does not identify in his argument for an offensive attitude and a continued solidarity between *us, Walloons and Brusselers*, the identity of the implied enemy leaves no doubt as the text prompts a reading within the framework of the national question. In the following article, the subject is a cultural issue, namely a film. Nevertheless, the article brings out the national issue quite explicitly.

Le Soir's Version of the Current Cultural Situation in Today's Belgium[47]

(6) The Flemish Oscar candidate goes to Namur![48]

The article was printed in the section *Actualité culturelle* (*Le Soir*, 26 March 2001). An introductory paragraph informs the reader that, on the initiative of the Minister of Cultural Affairs, Rudy Demotte, the film *Iedereen Beroemd*[49] will be shown at different venues in Wallonia from March 28 to March 31 concurrently with the Motion Picture Awards Party in Hollywood. Dominique Deruddere's film was nominated for the award for Best Foreign Film. After this factual piece of information, an article placed under the heading 'HUMEUR' follows under the above headline, "The Flemish Oscar candidate goes to Namur!" It reports on a dinner cocktail party on Sunday at Namur, the capital of Wallonia, given by the Minister of Culture.

From the very beginning, the tone is set by the exclamation mark and the first sentence: "The way to Hell is paved with good intentions…"[50] The suggestive ellipsis points are the most eye-catching signal in the text, which employs an extremely expressive style that does little to conceal the journalist's disagreement with the minister's initiative. In addition to

---

47 "*l'actualité culturelle belge d'aujourd'hui*», cf. quotation below.
48 *HUMEUR L'oscarisable flamand va à Namur!*
49 *Everybody's Famous.*
50 *L'enfer est pavé de bonnes intentions…*

this first example, the text uses ellipsis points to express what it sees as scandalous: "A Hollywood-style party (…,) in honour of the film 'Iedereen Beroemd' by Deruddere, the Flemish Brusseler …".[51] Likewise, play on words is used: *tongue* and *language* having the same designation in French: "creating closer ties between artists on both sides of the language border (but it is a long time since the artists gave a damn about political dictates and they mix with their kindred spirits, whatever the … tongue"[52]. Once more, scandal is perceived to be afoot: "To parade his triumph Demotte invited the Flemish Minister of Culture, Bert Anciaux … who did not show up. But he did offer a reply per e-mail … in Dutch, which Demotte read aloud."[53] Emphasis is also employed: "Hasquin can flaunt his spleen in the Botanical Garden at Meise, which the Flemings recently have almost taken over…"[54] One might get the impression that the ellipsis points leave it to the reader to complete the sentences, but in fact there is no free choice, the substitutions are taken for granted; their only function being to stimulate the reader's indignation by the imputed scandal of a minister who fraternizes with the Flemings.

The journalist does not hesitate in demonstrating his position by exposing and condemning the Minister's gesture, which he calls 'naive': "Demotte's gesture is chivalrous and pracmatic, but in the current cultural situation in today's Belgium, it is naive."[55] He substantiates his judgement by the use of rhetorical questions displaying the minister's acts as a letdown of the Prime Minister of The French Community, the Brusseller Hasquin. The article concludes with the decree that "men of good intentions should resist their naive impulses"[56], repeating the rejection of the Minister's initiative.

---

51 *Une nuit hollywoodienne (…), en hommage au film « Iedereen Beroemd », du Bruxello-Flamand Deruddere…*
52 *resserrer les liens entre artistes des 2 bords linguistiques (mais les créateurs se moquent depuis longtemps des diktats politiciens et se voient selon des affinités qui n'ont rien à voir avec leurs… langues.*
53 *Pour marquer son coup, Demotte invita Bert Anciaux, ministre de la Culture flamande. Qui n'est… pas venu. Mais s'est fendu d'un courrier électronique en… néerlandais que Demotte a lu.*
54 *Hasquin pourra aller promener son spleen dans le Jardin botanique de Meise qui vient d'être quasiment conquis par les flamands…*
55 *Le geste de Demotte est chevaleresque et pragmatique. Mais naïf dans l'actualité culturelle belge d'aujourd'hui.*
56 *les hommes de bonne volonté doivent résister à des impulsions de fraîche candeur.*

The text constructs two clearly distinct groups, Francophones *vs.* Flemings. The Francophones,[57] to which the journalist belongs, (cf. *notre/ our*) are described by attributives that connote feelings: "The Francophones are often inclined to follow our (*sic*) hearts: they are brave and tolerant, but poor tacticians... and have the disastrous habit of offering their cheek only to get a slap."[58] The Flemings[59], in contrast, are described as conquerors: "Anciaux, Volksunie has embarked on the conquest of Brussels"; "culture is a weapon of conquest for the Flemings".[60] To this conquest and the menace of Flemish hegemony, the Francophones are seen to oppose a battle of resistance. They perceive themselves, as well as Belgium, as victims: the partitioning to which our country is subjected.[61] *Dépeçage* seems to be a strong word (in comparison with words like division or even divorce). Although it must be granted that it is certainly only the time that is described as cynical and brutal, it seems obvious to extend this characterization to the conquering Flemings and their desire to exert hegemony.

This text, then, presents an undisguised construction of the Flemish group as the enemy of the Francophones and, further, of a conflict that sets the two groups in opposition to each other.

In a surprising and interesting way, the use of the term *belgitude* in the passage: "In a fit of Belgitude, which is still prevalent among the Francophones, although covert and melancholy, Rudy Demotte arranged (...)"[62] is out of line with the picture of Francophone open-mindedness and tolerance in matters of identity so far presented to *Le Soir*'s readers. *Belgitude* is rejected here as indication of a naive position and the text draws the lines of conflict with the Flemings, represented by Anciaux and his party, the nationalist Volksunie: the struggle about Brussels and the

---

57 Rudy Demotte, son collègue francophone; le ministre-président de la Communauté française Hasquin; le Bruxellois Hasquin; Happart, chantre catégorique de la résistance à l'hégémonie flandrienne.
58 *Les francophones penchent, souvent, du côté de notre cœur: ils sont braves, tolérants mais, peu tacticiens, (...) et ont la fâcheuse habitude de tendre la joue pour y attraper une baffe.*
59 Bert Anciaux, Volksunie.
60 *Anciaux, Volksunie lancé à la conquête de Bruxelles; la culture est une arme de conquête pour la Flandre.*
61 *le dépeçage dont notre pays est victime.*
62 *Rudy Demotte, saisi d'un élan de belgitude, encore majoritaire, même s'il est souterrain et mélancolique, chez les francophones, (...)*

Pathé-Palace, the Jardin botanique de Meise, the so-called *communes à facilités*, that are part of the region of Flanders, but where the Francophones have the right to be served in the French language. The text also reveals another conflict, which is immanent to the identity discourse of *Le Soir*.

Belgian Identity and "Belgitude" – Is there a Difference?

Our investigation started with a reference to the notion of belgitude as it was accounted for in the 1980 issue of Revue de l'Université de Bruxelles entitled "la belgique malgré tout" and it ends with a treatment of the criticism accusing Rudy Demotte of an ill-timed fit of belgitude. Instead of speaking of belgitude in the sense of the 1980s, when the term designated a "hollow feeling" of identity, which amounts to a non-definition, it seems that according to the 1998 article, one may again speak of a Belgian identity, indicating a sense of belonging. A cultivation of contacts between ministers of the two communities, however, seems to be inadmissible. According to Le Soir, the identity conflict that set the two communities in opposition to each other limits, or at least it should limit, according to *Le Soir*, the identification of the Francophones with Belgium.

In fact the term *belgitude* was coined to express and overcome the dilemma constituted by the need felt by Francophone Belgians for an identity and their inability to define themselves by reference to a Belgium that had recently been restructured (read: divided). However, what the two examples above show is precisely that they continue to identify themselves predominantly in relation to Belgium. In order to talk about this way of defining themselves, they often resort to the term *belgitude*. In *Le Soir*, it is used in a rather broad sense, ranging from a narrow historical meaning to an almost "banalized" usage, as it can be seen from the following examples from its columns.

Belgitude may be used to designate a specific way of being Belgian that incarnates the complexity of the country. A case in point is the singer-songwriter Marka, who, despite his Brussels background, lives in Flanders. He speaks the two languages fluently and uses both of them on the album dealt with: "With his engaged texts, Marka appears more serious than ever, the album opening with the multilingual song, 'Je parle', affirming his *belgitude* as a Brusseler living in Flanders and speaking both languages fluently."[63] (18 September 2001). Very often, however, *belgitude* simply refers to Belgium as a country without reference to her sub-entities such as the two communities or the three regions.[64] In this context, *belgitude* may correspond simply to a 'Belgian attachment' (*ancrage belge*) and thus refer more or less explicitly to Belgium before the federalization, to the Belgian nation-state. In the example "There goes another piece of *belgitude*, yet another! With the GIB group sale of its 15 Inno department stores to German Kaufhof, yet another piece of our economic heritage has been reflagged"[65] (21 April 2001), it is the expression 'our economic heritage' which manifests this dimension. Other articles refer explicitly to this pre-federal Belgium, *la Belgique de papa*, discussing initiatives to save the Belgian airline company Sabena using expressions such as *arch-Belgian* (*belgicain*) in *effort belgicain, voire de patriotisme* (10 November 2001); elsewhere in the same article it is contended that "we have parted with the idea expressed by 'belgian roots'". The two formulations hark back to the famous words attributed to Gaston Eyskens, Prime Minister 1968-1972: *La Belgique de papa a vécu*.[66] The words, which are said to have been pronounced in 1970, have since formed part of the collective imagery of the Belgians.

The **'hegemonic'** discourse that has been documented by the analyses of the *Le Soir* articles refers to a hegemony that is contested, but which persistently seeks to articulate and thus maintain a common identity. To achieve this goal, it mixes notions transcending the national identity[67] and notions that unambiguously belong to the national Belgian imagery such

---

63 *Marka se révèle plus grave que jamais avec des textes soucieux, l'album s'ouvrant par le «Je parle» polyglotte affirmant sa belgitude de Bruxellois vivant en Flandre et parlant couramment les deux langues.*
64 Though there are in fact three communities, I deliberately speak of two only, as the last one, the German speaking community, does not occur in my material from *Le Soir*. This absence is characteristic of the newspaper's identity discourse, witness the text on "Iedereen Beroemd" (6).
65 *Et un morceau de belgitude en moins, un! Avec la vente par le groupe GIB de ses quinze grands magasins Inno à l'allemand Kaufhof, c'est une nouvelle part de notre patrimoine économique qui passe sous pavillon étranger.*
66 The authenticity of these words is contested, cf. André Mean, the journalist and specialist of communitarian problems in Belgium, in *La Belgique de papa*, Bruxelles, Politique & Histoire, 1989.
67 *un pays mosaïque, une Belgique plurielle, bigarrée, métissée.*

as the stereotyped self-image: "the cultural ambassadors, such as Magritte and Broodthaers, Masters of Belgitude, of typical Belgian irony"[68] (7 March 2001); "potato chips are as much a symbol of Belgium as is Eddy Merckx"[69] (16 February 2001). The first belong to the "cultural *belgitude*", as do Brel, Hergé and Tintin. The symbolic value of a hero like Eddy Merckx and sport heroes in general is well known; also when speaking of them, *Le Soir* does not hesitate to use the term *belgitude*: "On a wave of *belgitude*, with some sexual fantasies thrown in, the Juju phenomenon attracts a public which is totally foreign to the tennis game"[70] (of Justine Henin, 17 July 2001); "Wallonia happily pays tribute to his belgitude"[71] (of Joël Smets, who had been awarded the *Trophée du mérite sportif* and the title *Sportif belge de l'année*, 15 March, 2001). In other words, *belgitude* is a floating signifier whose meaning depends on situation and context. The very broad and banalized usage of the term when speaking of sports, the marketplace, commerce and industry seems to be an aspect of the *Le Soir* discourse, *belgitude* coming to be the equivalent of Belgian identity as a national identity and thus fulfil a need for an identity that seems to survive despite the dissolution of the nation-state, i.e. the federalization, the very process which it seeks to deny.

This integrating and homogenizing identity discourse is, however, unable to eliminate the antagonisms within Belgian society, if this can still be said to exist. It collides with reality, i.e. the particularism of Flanders and its own particularism. The bicultural sector is one of the areas where this collision can be witnessed. The importance attributed to this sector by *Le Soir* shows us that it is an element of the identity constructed by this discourse, i.e. an element of what is perceived as specifically Belgian, but an element which Flanders wishes to appropriate as an element of the Flemish specificity.

---

68 *les ambassadeurs culturels [Magritte, Broodthaers], les maîtres ès belgitude, ès ironie-typiquement-belge.*
69 *la frite est un emblème aussi belge qu'Eddy Merckx.* This passage continues: *Cela n'étonnera personne : il y a même un site 100% belgitude qui répond à www.frites.be.* Another article asks this question: *La frite est-elle un élément ontologique de la belgitude?* (8 May, 2001).
70 *Sur une vague de belgitude, avec quelques fantasmes sexuels en prime, le phénomène Juju attire un public tout à fait profane en tennis.*
71 *La Wallonie rend volontiers hommage à sa belgitude.*

In a historical perspective, the present situation in Belgium may be understood as the result of a process of a "contextual unification of a system of differences [that] can only take place at the price of weakening the purely differential identities" and that was the expression of "something present in each of them (...), which was opposition to the regime."[72] In the process that led to the foundation of Belgium, the regime referred to was that of the Dutch king. Once independence had been achieved, the "sliding of the signified under the signifier"[73] continued and led to what *Le Soir* has called "the strange tranquil earthquake that the country underwent at its 150th anniversary"[74] (13 January 2001), viz. the federalization of the country and the demise of the old Belgium, 'la Belgique de papa'. It is this 'pre-federal' hegemonic discourse (leading to a hegemony of the empty signifiers of the 'nation' and 'the people') that we may still witness in the columns of *Le Soir*. It does not only lend a particular content to the elements of the discourse, but it distinguishes as well between different types of nationalism. In this context, one might refer to Balibar's definition of "a 'thin' and 'good' nationalism that is based on right and constructs nations in terms of formal political communities (*Gesellschaft*) and, on the other hand, a 'thick' and 'bad' nationalism that is based on might and destroys nations – either from the inside (separatism) or from the outside (imperialism) – in the name of the superior virtues of an organic community (*Gemeinschaft*)."[75] Obviously the definition of 'thick' and 'bad' nationalism applies to a Flemish nationalism (which is both separatist and conquering) as well as Walloon claims of an identity and for further autonomy as presented in *Le Soir*.[76] Though the newspaper's conception of a Belgian identity is presented as a contrast to such nationalist visions, it does not conform to Balibar's definition of a politically framed 'thin' and 'good' nationalism. This is due to two factors. Firstly, it does not stress the rational political aspects of the nation-state, but rather the emotional

---

72 Laclau, 1996:54.
73 Laclau, 2000:27.
74 *étrange séisme pacifique que le pays traversa au tournant de son siècle et demi d'existence.*
75 Balibar, 1991a:47; quoted from Torfing, 1999:195.
76 The Walloons themselves, on the contrary, often think their claims in terms of the political *Gesellschaft*-model, cf. Degn,1999:108-109.

aspects of identity and belonging. Secondly, the stigmatization of the Flemings as separatists and conquerors seizing upon goods that rightly belong to others, and the inferiorization and minimization of the Walloons (by identifying them with debts, folklore and the "ridiculous Van Cau") are far more emotional than rational. It might even be suggested that their hatred of the Flemings and the declared Walloons could be explained as a hatred of their own obsessive relationship with their nation.[77]

Conclusion

The lines of fracture dividing the Belgian nation-state, which are institutionalised in the federal constitution and manifest themselves in identity conflicts and competing claims, are clearly reflected in the identity debate, as it appears from the selection of texts analysed here. What we are witnessing is an identity discourse that seeks to maintain a Belgian identity and seeks to do this by a hegemonic discourse that fixes the meaning both of the Belgian identity and of the competing identities. As part of its hegemonizing of the nodal points of this discourse, *Le Soir* transmits and supports discourses that may help to construct a Belgian identity capable of encompassing and integrating a multiplicity of identities. This is done by means of chains of equivalence, as e.g. when Belgian identity is described as a multiple, multicoloured, mixed, vital mosaic (*une identité mosaïque, plurielle, bigarrée, métissée, vivante*), etc. This universalizing image of an identity seeking at the same time to justify itself as tolerant and open, and to stigmatize as nationalist those identity discourses that contradict it. By rejecting the others' particularism and nationalism, it seeks to mitigate its own particularism and nationalism.

---

77 This consideration is based on Torfing, 1999: Chapter 10.

A QUEST FOR DIALOGISM
looking back at Italian political violence in the '70s

Francesco Caviglia and Leonardo Cecchini

INTRODUCTION

The wave of political violence in the '70s is still an open question in recent Italian history. No public Commission for Truth and Reconciliation has been established by the political system, but there exists a huge number of memoirs, interviews and fictional works with political violence as the central theme. However, public discourse on terrorism, present or past, is in Italy plagued by monovocality, or rather by a plurality of voices without dialogue.

The almost unconscious ambition we had at the beginning of our research was to find evidence for suggesting that truth and reconciliation was possible and that maybe dialogue was already firmly established and only needed to be made more visible, for example in school textbooks. Coming from a background in literary and cultural studies and with the example of fiction about the Vietnam war or German terrorism in mind, we also proposed a working hypothesis that fiction might often prove more polyphonic and dialogical – in the Bakhtinian sense – than not-fiction, and therefore prove effective for historical understanding and as a contribution to debate. On the basis of these premises we set out to look for polyphonic, dialogic contributions both in fiction and in non-fiction, across different genres and media. We did find some examples, although these were far fewer than we had expected. Our attention shifted then towards understanding what made these examples especially effective – in our eyes – for promoting dialogic discursive practice.

This paper will start by describing the historical background of this search and the condition of split memory and monologism that afflicts public discourse. In the second part, after a brief outline of the concept of dialogism, we will present and analyse the discursive practice reflected and constructed by two examples – an interview and a fictional film – that we believe make valid contributions to understanding and overcoming terrorism.

The background: political violence in Italy in the '70s

Between 1969 and the late '80s Italy was afflicted by a wave of terrorist attacks inspired by both left-wing and right-wing ideologies; these were far more extensive than in other European countries and resulted in a high death toll.

Right-wing terrorism, which claimed the largest number of victims, was a "classic" form of terrorism that aimed to spread terror by planting bombs in crowded places without claiming responsibility. This terrorism received backing from members of key institutions (including the police, the judiciary and especially the intelligence services) and from "invisible powers" (such as the P2 Masonic lodge and other secret and illegal organizations); the aim was to block the democratic redistribution of power and shift the political system towards the right (the so-called strategia della tensione, see for example De Lutiis, 1996).

By contrast, left-wing terrorism had its roots in the '68 protest movement, which saw social and political struggle for the democratization and modernization of Italian society. At the beginning of the '70s, a few extreme left-wing groups carried out illegal but initially bloodless propaganda acts, which they called lotta armata, or "armed struggle". Initially, these actions encountered some complicity and sympathy in a minority within the working class and the student movement,[1] but this support was later to evaporate when the Red Brigades kidnapped and murdered the Christian Democrat politician Aldo Moro in 1978, and, more generally, when the lotta armata turned into a sequence of assassinations whose victims were politicians, policemen, judges, industrialists and journalists.

By the mid '80s, left-wing terrorism was defeated, and the defeat was recognised in public declarations by the terrorists themselves. But the wave of terrorism in the '70s remains an open wound in Italian society. Establishing a kind of shared memory is difficult not only because of the sorrow and high toll of human lives, but also because of the complexity of the political and social clashes in those years. In Italy in the '70s two opposing form of terrorism were present, each with its own political agenda: right-wing terrorism had a conspirative character and enjoyed the complicity of members of the political establishment while left-wing terrorism was characterized by a blend of ideological fanaticism, revolutionary mythology but also aspirations to overcome the stalemate in the political system (aspirations which were shared by many Italians and which left-wing terrorism was also responsible for thwarting).

Looking back in anger: split memory, conflicting discourses

After the fall of the Berlin wall, the collapse of Italy's Christian Democrat dominated political system, and the dawn of a new era in Italian public life following the realisation that the "state of emergency" (as the period 1969-89 is usually called in Italy) was over, some attempts have been made to move towards a form of "reconciliation". The debate was slow to take off in the '90s but gradually gained momentum, with many concurring and conflicting voices in the public arena, but also with some official steps

---

1 The number of left-wing terrorists in the period 1969-89 is estimated at about ten thousand (with an area of about one hundred thousand sympathizers), but about one million persons may have been involved in some form of left-wing subversion in the same period.

taken by institutions of the State.² More recently, however, the assassinations of two trade union consultants carried out in 1999 and in March 2002 by the so-called "new" Red Brigades, and also the 11th September 2001 attack have effectively put the lid on all these attempts.

Still, there is a need to move on, to start healing the traumas and lacerations of those years when democracy itself was in danger in Italy. But dialogue, which is a precondition for any future, more circumstantially historical reconstruction of the period, is not flourishing.

Different demands (psychological, political, ethical and so on) are mixed together in Italian public opinion about the political violence of the recent past: sorrow and feelings of vendetta; the need to forgive, but also fear that forgiving will mean forgetting; the need to forget the past and get a long awaited "sign of pacification"; the difficulty of doing that; acknowledgement that the judicial rulings on the "state of emergency" do not of themselves bring about equity. It hardly comes as a surprise that all these positions are usually in sharp contrast with each other; the real problem, however, is that these discourses tend to be monological and insensitive to the reasons of the Other.

The most hegemonic discourse in public opinion is the so-called "judiciary discourse", which represents the opinion of the majority of the people. It looks at terrorists as criminals and totally disregard terrorism's political and social motivations; "lock them up and throw away the key" as a character of film La seconda volta (1996, The second time) puts it.

But also at the judicial level things are not straightforward. The judicial system had a crucial role in defeating terrorism without compromising democracy (many Italians at that time called for court martials and the death penalty) thanks to the so-called legge sui pentiti ('law on repentant offenders', an interestingly religious terminology for the equivalent of 'crown witnesses', or supergrasses as they're known in Ireland), which still rewards collaboration with substantial reductions in prison terms. But

---

2 On July 29, 1997 the Judiciary Committee of the Italian Parliament began discussing a law that would reduce the punishment of terrorists imprisoned for crimes committed up to 1989. In the same year, President of the Republic Oscar Luigi Scalfaro issued a pardon to six terrorists who had been long imprisoned and who had never actually killed or shot anyone.

the price to pay was often injustice, such as the setting free of terrorists responsible for many murders, while simple militants with little of importance to reveal have been given long jail sentences. It was not easy for the relatives of the victims to see their father's, son's, husband's murderers go free because they were pentiti.

The judiciary discourse has determined the categories used for classifying the present-day position of former terrorists: the "repentants", that is those who gave evidence for the state; the dissociati (dissociated), those who "only" distanced themselves from terrorism; and those who did neither and were classified as irriducibili, "unrepentent". This distinction is laid down in criminal records and in media reports, but may be in blatant contradiction with the actual position that the accused hold about terrorism: for example irriducibile Nadia Ponti always refused to undertake any public act that might lighten her sentence, but from jail wrote a quite radical criticism of her experience in the lotta armata (Ponti, 1997), while as a free man dissociato Corrado Alunni wrote in quite apologetic and even nostalgic terms about his group, one with the highest number of victims (Alunni, 2001).

On the political scene a few voices have acknowledged that the new historical situation calls for reconciliation and that Italy is now ready to close the book on terrorism. According to Francesco Cossiga, Home Minister at the time of the Moro kidnapping and former President of the Republic, the period 1969-89 was a kind of civil war in which the State played dirty too with secret conspiracies; we shall let bygones be bygones and move on, he said. Cossiga publicly recognized that left-wing terrorism was socially and politically motivated, acknowledged the status of former terrorists as "political prisoners" and then proposed a collective amnesty for them,[3] possibly – according to his critics – to prevent possible inquiries into the role of State institutions and invisible powers in this war. Cossiga's position is not widely shared. Victims of terrorism and/or their

---

3 Cossiga first proposed an amnesty in July 1991, during his presidency. In November 1991 he visited the former leader of the Red Brigades Renato Curcio in prison.

relatives in particular already feel abandoned by the State and are not ready to accept a "forgive and forget" policy.

On the other hand, some victims accepted to meet those who had injured them or who had murdered their beloved, and personally forgave them, but they have also publicly declared that pardon is an individual act which concerns the individual conscience of each victim; accordingly, they would not approve of an amnesty (a collective pardon) from the State, but possibly only "grazia", that is a pardon granted exclusively by the President of the Republic to single terrorists with due respect to the individual profile of each single offender.[4] As a form of compromise, in an attempt to acknowledge terrorism's political and social motivations (Cossiga's "civil war" aspect) without erasing the juridical responsibility of the acts committed by each single terrorist, the possibility has been discussed of an "indulto", a particular form of pardon which only reduces the prisoner's remaining imprisonment (during "the state of emergency", laws were introduced that increased punishment for crimes of terrorism).

There is similar diversity in the positions of former terrorists.[5] Many, after a public repudiation of political violence, only want to forget and be forgotten, and after they have served their time they want to live as normal a life as possible. Others (especially some former leaders who have published books about their experience as terrorists) try to justify their past in many ways.

For example, the former leader of Red Brigates, Renato Curcio, when asked who gave him the right to kill, dodged the question by comparing his responsibility with that of the "generations of our fathers and grandfathers", which produced many more casualties than terrorists, and concluded: "the generosity that a part of my generation has shown in the political-ideological struggle represents a positive value which one day

---

4 Adolfo Bachelet publicly forgave Anna Laura Braghetti of the Red Brigades who was responsible for murdering his brother Vittorio (see Braghetti's account in her *Il prigioniero*, 1998). Architect Sergio Lenci met in prison Giulia Borelli who shot him in 1980. He still has the bullet in his head and his account (*Colpo alla nuca*, 1988) inspired Mimmo Calopresti's film *La seconda volta*.
5 A number of them are still in prison but benefit from the so called Gozzini law, which under given conditions grants long-term convicts permission to work outside of prison.

will have to be recognized"[6] (Curcio, 1993: 212). This statement sounds to us like an insane plea for recognition at any cost, and we agree with Carol Beebe Tarantelli (the widow of the economist Ezio Tarantelli, one of the latest victims of Red Brigates) when she attributes Curcio's failure to comprehend the tragic consequences of his words and acts to paranoia and delirium of omnipotence (Tarantelli, 1999).

DIALOGUE AS A PRECONDITION FOR UNDERSTANDING: A NOTE ON METHOD

As we see, the different positions actively contradict each other most of the time, and all this in a society which is already split on many issues. It is no wonder that a monologic tonality is prevailing among all these discourses. Many of the people involved in debate have a big personal stake in terms of freedom, identity, votes they suppose to get or lose by sustaining a given position. As a consequence, the few voices trying to establish dialogue have often been submerged by the prevailing tones of the debate, with the result that there is no shared understanding of terrorism in the '70s. Although this is difficult to prove, the recent resurgence of left-wing terrorism might not be extraneous to this lack of collective elaboration, which has made it possible for marginal fringes to consider former terrorists as heroes to imitate.

In looking for discourses which might foster a better understanding, we have taken dialogue as the only possible way to achieve knowledge of a (human) subject, as defined by Bakhtin (1986: 161) and further explained by Todorov (1981). In particular, we have recognized the higher or lower dialogism of the different texts and discourses on the basis of two elements: the representation of the Other and the relation established with the partner in communication.

We include with the first term Bakhtin's polyphony ("a plurality of consciousnesses, with equal rights, each with its own world, combining

---

[6] La generosità con cui una fetta della mia generazione si è gettata nella rischiosa avventura politico-ideologica rappresenta un valore positivo che, a un certo punto, dovrà esserci riconosciuto.

the unity of an event but nonetheless without fusing"; Bakhtin 1984: 6), as well as vnenakhodimost or 'exotopy' ('finding oneself outside', as explained and translated by Todorov 1984: 99) as the act – performed in this passage within the realm of artistic creativity – of encompassing the other as "an elsewhere beyond integration or reduction":

> No fusion with the other but the preservation of his [the writer's] exotopic position and of his excess of vision and comprehension, that is its correlative. But the question arises as to how Dostoevsky uses this surplus. Not for objectivation or completion. The most important moment of this surplus is love (one cannot love oneself, it is a coordinated relation); then, confession, forgiveness (the conversation between Stavrogin and Tikhon), finally an active understanding (that does not reduplicate), watchful listening (quotation from Todorov, 1984: 106, original italics, our underline; the whole essay in Bakhtin, 1984, Appendix II).

This attitude does not mean accepting all positions as equally valid:

> Our point of view is not at all tantamount to asserting a kind of passivity on the part of the author, who could confine himself to making a montage of the viewpoints of others, of the truths of others, and would surrender altogether his own viewpoint, his truth. That is not at all the case; rather, it is a case of an entirely new and specific interrelation between his truth and the truth of someone else. The author is profoundly active, but his action takes on a specific dialogic character [...] Dostoevsky frequently interrupts the other's voice, but he does not cover it up, he never finishes it from the "self", that is from an alien consciousness (his own) (id., p. 106).

A model of this attitude outside literature is Todorov's watchful listening to different points of view and value systems from the discovery and conquest of America, from the siege of the Warsaw ghetto or from occupied France (Todorov, 1982, 1991, 1995). As for the relationship established between the partners in dialogue, we wish to incorporate into Bakhtin's dialogical principle the notion of strategies of involvement in discourse of the listener or reader as the driving element of discourse, as developed especially by Chafe (1985:116) and Tannen (1984, 1989, 1992, 1997)[7].

The next two sections will show these concepts at work in two examples: an interview with a former terrorist and a fictional film about the encounter between a victim of terrorism and the woman who had shot him ten years before.

Dialogue at work: an interview with former terrorist Silveria Russo

Curcio in his book-interview seems fundamentally unable to recognize the reasons of the Other: his style of argument has a rather stringent logic in examining different options, but he has obvious difficulties in considering points of view that are radically different from his own.

A quite different attitude is revealed in an interview with another former terrorist, Silveria Russo: here a polyphonic discourse reveals an attempt to understand and make the other understand. The interview was part of a TV program, La notte della Repubblica (The Night of the Republic), by journalist Sergio Zavoli and broadcast- by the Italian state broadcaster, RAI, in the early '90s, in our view the best TV program so far produced about the so-called "anni di piombo"[8] and still a model for the documentary genre in Italy.

At the time of the interview, Silveria Russo, who was involved in planning and carrying out at least two murders, had been in jail for almost 10 years. In prison she distanced herself from terrorism, confessed the crimes she had committed, but did not turn in other comrades. Today she is free, has two sons and works for an organisation for the care of aged

---

7   [if applies] See also in this volume Caviglia, Crime news at school: a challenge for critical literacy.
8   This is another common way to designate in Italy the period 1969-98 and it comes from the Italian title of Margarethe Von Trotta's film *Die bleierne Zeit* ("The Leaden years", 1981, known as *The German sisters* or *Marianne and Julienne*). *Bleierne Zeit* actually refers in von Trotta's film to the '50s in Germany, but in Italy the title was appropriated – through association with the lead of the bullets – to describe the late '70s.

people. Our analysis is based on a written transcription of her interview (in Zavoli, 1992: 373-85).[9]

Silveria Russo has reflected on her experience and undergone a transformation. This development is revealed in a discontinuity in language, where the ideological discourse of her former self is still reflected in her account of her life as a terrorist and set against her current beliefs. Some examples: In her "yesterday voice" the terrorist group is an "armed organisation" (organizzazione armata), the group's members are "comrades" (compagni), the activity of attacking and killing people is called "armed actions" (azioni armate), "direct action on a man" (azione diretta su un uomo) and seen as "normal operative activity" (normale attività operativa). In this voice the reasons for an "action" and for "armed struggle" in general are expressed in a language that encapsulates would-be revolutionary practice into the worst tradition of vagueness in Italian political discourse: becoming a terrorist means "carrying on a discourse of armed struggle" (portare avanti un discorso di lotta armata) and killing a female prison officer "was part of the discourse we were carrying on in that moment" (faceva parte del discorso che stavamo portando avanti in quell momento).

Even more abstract and abstruse is the language Silveria Russo uses to explain the reason why she and her group decided to kill democratic and left-wing judge Guido Galli (Zavoli, 1992: 383-84); this language is blatantly contradicted by her new voice expressed with the most simple words, when she explains what she recognized later: Judge Galli era un uomo buono ("was a good, decent man"). Silveria Russo's present-day voice acknowledges that the "actions" were terrorism (she speaks of "wave of terrorism", ondata terroristica) and "murder" (l'omicidio Lorusso) and admits that an action (killing a bartender who had recognized some terrorists and called the police) was simply a vendetta, a word that could not be more extraneous to the language of political struggle. The distance

---

9 A selection of interviews from the TV-program has recently been published on videotape, but Silveria Russo's interview was not included in the choice. It seems that the editors were more interested in interviews with former terrorist leaders (it is also possible that some of the persons interviewed were no longer willing, ten years later, to return to the public arena; but we have no information about the editorial history of the video edition).

Silveria Russo perceives from the past emerges as well in utterances such as "the work – let's call it that way – of the terrorist" (il lavoro, chiamiamolo pure così, del terrorista).

The schizophrenia between the two languages is possibly the best clue to understanding an unsettling concept: that resorting to political violence "was in the order of things" (era nell'ordine delle cose) for a small but significant fragment of the Italian left-wing movement in the '70s. This concept is clearly present in many of the different points of view on terrorism seen in the Section 3, but is often proposed either as a good excuse for having become a terrorist ("we had the courage to do what others only talked about", a position held for example by Curcio) or else seen as a proof of the intrinsically Stalinist character of the Italian left-wing in general.

Silveria Russo and interviewer Sergio Zavoli manage instead to reveal that an otherwise normal person who cares for her loved ones (a husband, a dog) can at the same time be a killer, and that the same person can see later the absurdity of her choice and even demystify an explanation of terrorism in purely political terms. She acknowledges the blinding role of ideological discourse in the decision process of killing ("people were symbols, not human beings"), but speaks at the same time of even less noble "protagonism within the group" and competition between groups as a significant cause of actions.

In his Bakhtinian watchful listening, Sergio Zavoli deserves in our view big credit for the result of this interview. He is neither a judge nor an accomplice, but is not by any means indifferent. As we understand it, Zavoli had two main items on his agenda: to show that former terrorists are human beings and not monsters, as largely held by public opinion at the end of the '80s, and to expose how their actions did great harm to other human beings who did not deserve it. But it is the viewer's responsibility to draw this conclusion, Zavoli never lectures anybody. Which does not mean he accepts everything. For example, the only time he interrupts Silveria Russo is while she is describing an "action" in which her group ambushed a squad of policemen; in the shoot-out a passer-by was also killed. As Silveria Russo merely hints at this victim as an unwanted casualty, Zavoli reminds her that "that person – pardon me – was a 13 year old boy" (quella persona, mi scusi, era un ragazzo di 13 anni). It's a shame we cannot hear Sergio Zavoli's tone of voice, which probably – together with "pardon me" – helped soften the painful remark. We would translate his meta-message as "I know I am saying something painful for you and I'm sorry, but this victim too deserves to be mentioned and mourned by me, by you and by the viewers". Silveria Russo at least seems to understand the remark in these terms, as the dialogue and even trust which has been built up between the two is not disrupted, and the interview proceeds.

In summary, dialogism in this interview involves all the actors in the scene: Silveria Russo, who manages to give voice to her previous and present selves; Sergio Zavoli, with his attitude of listening and steering conversation only when necessary; the viewer, who is required, and is trusted, to be able to make sense of the whole.

Another dialogic option: La seconda volta by Mimmo Calopresti

Confrontation with the past is represented in a different way in Mimmo Calopresti's film La seconda volta (1996). The title is an explicit reference to the theme of the film: a latter-day encounter between victim and victimizer.[10]

One of the two main characters in the film, the university lecturer Alberto Sajevo (played by actor and director Nanni Moretti), had been shot by left wing terrorists ten years before, at a time when he was responsible for job lay-offs at Fiat, and he still has a (in some ways symbolic) bullet in the head. His life stopped at that moment: his marriage broke down and his private life is now a wreck, with his younger sister as his only social contact. Lisa Venturi, the other main character in the film, is the terrorist who shot him. After spending 10 years in jail, she has now started work outside on day release, returning to prison at night (accord-

---

10 Our analysis is also based on the unpublished script of *La seconda volta*, provided by courtesy of scriptwriter Francesco Bruni.

ing to a program for the rehabilitation of convicts). Alberto meets her by chance; she fails to recognize him[11] and he starts to follow her obsessively (ironically, in the same way left wing terrorists stalked their victims before the attack).

Disguised behind a romantic interest (he sends her flowers), Alberto's obsessive involvement with Lisa is aimed at obtaining some kind of retribution. To his sister who asks him why he didn't immediately reveal who he was, he answers: "I couldn't. The first time I talked to her she didn't even recognize me. Do you understand what that means? It means I haven't existed for all these years. Cancelled. Removed."[12] Half way through the film he reveals his real identity to her and confronts her with her past actions, but Lisa runs away from him without saying anything and refuses to talk to him later, when he tries to visit her in prison. For a period she even refuses the privilege of working outside.

It is only at the very end of the film that Lisa, instead of going back to prison after work, decides to visit Alberto and confront his questions. As we will see, this final encounter does not end up with a formal reconciliation, but makes it possible for both of them to advance their understanding of the other's condition.

Alberto has an absolutely monological voice as 'victim' and, understandably enough, has no sympathy with any argument for a reconciliation with former terrorists. He is vociferously annoyed by outspoken former terrorists publishing books and giving interviews, as in the scene where he reads aloud the same passage from Curcio's memoirs which we mentioned above. He is still traumatized and has never consented to the removal of the bullet from his head, which makes him the emblem

---

11 According to former Red Brigade member Alberto Franceschini, not recognizing one's victim is quite unlikely (Franceschini, 1995); but according to other terrorists' memoirs this is a commonly feared possibility (Braghetti & Mambro, 1995: 162).

12 "Non ci sono riuscito. Quando le ho parlato per la prima volta non mi ha neanche riconosciuto. Sai che cosa significa? Che in tutti questi anni io per lei non sono esistito. Cancellato, rimosso". (La seconda volta, screenplay, Scene 64).

of Italian society unable to liberate itself from the wounds of terrorism (O'Leary, 2002:37).[13]

Lisa, on the other hand, looks like a quite normal person who is leading a calm and solitary life: working out, sleeping in prison and with few dedicated friendships. She too is in a kind of limbo, a state of suspension that originates from the desire to forget and be forgotten, as experienced by many former terrorists. She says to her cellmate in prison: "I would like to sleep my whole life long" (vorrei dormire tutta una vita).

A large part of the film is devoted to showing Alberto and Lisa in their everyday lives; the viewer becomes acquainted with them and their condition. They are not especially likeable, in particular Alberto, but it is evident that they are still suffering for something that for most of us is a faint memory. The film's slow tempo encourages the viewer to compare his/her own last ten years of life with the non-life of the two main characters.

We will focus now on the last encounter of Lisa and Alberto at the end of the film.

This happens months after the first casual meeting with Lisa, at that moment in which Alberto has decided to undergo surgery in a clinic abroad to have the bullet removed from his head. He had also decided to move to another apartment (this second decision is symbolic too, since Alberto, after his divorce, has continued living in the same apartment where he had been shot). Lisa rings at his door the day before Alberto is due to leave for the operation. The first minutes of the encounter are devoted to formal courtesy, small-talk and preparing coffee. In the original script, at this point Alberto asks Lisa to tell him how she shot him. She repeats, rather quietly, the same details she gave at the trial, with Alberto in an attitude of watchful listening. The whole confession was dropped from the final version of the film, adding further ellipsis to the scene and requiring the viewer to figure out the most intimate part of the dialogue.

---

13 See also the strongly symbolic scene where Alberto is rowing slowly in an indoor pool mumbling the Red Brigades's slogan "*Colpirne uno per educarne cento*" (to hit one is to educate a hundred). Alberto is making movement without actually making any progress; that is, he is still prisoner of the events of the past.

The director cuts instead to Alberto's sister talking worriedly with her partner about the effect the encounter may have on Alberto, and then to the parole judge receiving notice that Lisa did not come back to prison after work and that she has become, technically speaking, a fugitive.

When the camera returns to Alberto and Lisa they are outside, walking together. Lisa's voice is more relaxed, now. Involvement between them is mediated by the details she gives him as a sort of gift, and dialogue seems possible, as in the following scene (parts of the script omitted in the film are in square brackets):

Scene 88. Lisa and Alberto are walking side by side on a boulevard along the river.

LISA: [... ero a casa, un appartamento che dividevo con altre due ragazze. Mi ricordo che pioveva a dirotto.] Avevo appena dato il primo esame. [Semiologia.] Era anche andato bene. È passato questo ragazzo, Gianni, di Milano. L'avevo conosciuto quel giorno stesso in una manifestazione. Aveva una pistola e mi ha chiesto se gliela potevo tenere a casa mia.

ALBERTO: E lei accettò.

LISA: Sì. Mi sembrava naturale. In quella manifestazione la polizia aveva ucciso uno studente. Lo guarda, prima di proseguire: Una settimana dopo Gianni mi telefonò e voleva che gli portassi la pistola in una casa fuori città, che usava come base. Io ci andai, e ci rimasi. Una mattina la polizia fece una perquisizione: noi non c'eravamo, ma trovarono i miei documenti. Da quel giorno mi ritrovai in clandestinità.

ALBERTO: Insomma, successe tutto per caso.

LISA: No. Immagino che prima o poi lo avrei fatto comunque.

LISA: [I was at home, in an apartment I shared with two other girls. I remember it was pouring.] I had just passed my first examination. [Semiology.] It even went well. This guy came by, Gianni, from Milan. I had first met him that very day at a demonstration. He had a gun. He asked if I could hide it at my place.

ALBERTO: And you accepted.

LISA: Yes. It seemed natural to me. During that demonstration the police had killed a student.
She looks at him, then adds:
One week later Gianni called and asked me to bring the gun to a house outside town he used as a hideout. I went there, and stayed. One morning the police searched the house: we were not there, but they found my ID card. From that day I had to go into hiding.

ALBERTO: You mean, everything happened by chance.

LISA: No. I guess I would have done it anyway, sooner or later.

Alberto is struck by the contrast between Lisa's idea that becoming a terrorist was "in the order of things" and the harmless appearance of the young woman he is talking to. There is another cut in the sequence and then political discourse breaks in and disrupts the dialogue:

Scene 90. A bar

ALBERTO: E allora, perché avete scelto proprio me?	ALBERTO: So why was it me you chose?
LISA: Lo sa.	LISA: You know why.
ALBERTO: Lo so? Non mi conoscevate, non sapevate nemmeno che faccia avessi. Mi odiavate così tanto da volermi uccidere. Perché? La guarda per invitarla a parlare, ma Lisa è chiusa nel suo mutismo. "Colpirne uno per educarne cento." Dove sono i cento che avete educato colpendo me?	ALBERTO: Do I? You didn't know me, you didn't even know what I looked like. And yet, you hated me so much you wanted to kill me. He looks at her, but she remains silent. " Hit one and educate 100". Where are the hundred you have educated by hitting me?
LISA (con uno scatto improvviso): Sono parole che non hanno più senso. È questo che vuole sentirsi dire? Che ho rovinato la mia vita per una cosa che non ha più senso?	LISA (Bursting out): These words don't make sense any more. Is this what you want to hear from me? That I ruined my life for something that doesn't make sense any more?
ALBERTO: La sua e la mia vita per una cosa che non aveva senso neanche allora.	ALBERTO: Your life and mine, for something that has never made sense.
LISA: Questo non può dirlo nessuno.	LISA: Nobody can judge that.
ALBERTO: Io lo dico, invece. E sa perché? Perché le cose che volevate cambiare sono andate avanti come prima, forse peggio. Ed è stata anche colpa vostra.	ALBERTO: I do. Want to know why? Because the things you wanted to change carried on as before, maybe even got worse. And it was partly your fault.
LISA: Cosa sta dicendo? Erano in molti a chiederci di fare quello che abbiamo fatto. E lei lo sa benissimo.	LISA: What are you saying? There were many who were asking us to do what we did. And you know that well.
ALBERTO: Va be', se lei vuol continuare a credere a queste cazzate, mi sa che qui stiamo proprio perdendo tempo. Lisa non replica. Alberto sorride amaro.	ALBERTO: Well, if you want to keep believing this bullshit, I'm afraid we're wasting our time. Lisa does not reply. Alberto smiles bitterly.
LISA: C'è un telefono qui? Chiamo un taxi.	LISA: Is there a phone here. I've got to call a cab.
ALBERTO: E' lì.	ALBERTO: It's over there.

In this exchange, Alberto makes a crude (and quite reasonable) political analysis of terrorism.

Lisa does not want to talk about it, but feeling cornered she falls back to identitarian discourse, using the same arguments adopted in books written by former terrorists such as Curcio. Maybe she suspects that Alberto is right, or maybe not: it is up to the viewer to translate her silence. At any rate, when Lisa and Alberto's conversation melts into public political debate there is no room for dialogue: talking becomes a waste of time.

But there is one last scene in their encounter. Alberto accompanies Lisa outside, waiting for the taxi. The atmosphere between them now is colder after the last exchange, but dialogue will be resumed on a different plane (our notes are in bold italics, within square brackets).

Scene 90. Outside, night. [waiting for the taxi]	
ALBERTO: Va a Bologna?	Are you going to Bologna?
[Alberto remembers that Lisa's parents live in Bologna and believes she is on weekend leave from prison]	
Lisa esita un momento: LISA: Sì.	Lisa hesitates for a moment: LISA: Yes.
[she is lying, she should be back in prison now; she will be punished for not returning]	
Dopo una pausa, chiede: LISA: Anche lei è in partenza?	After a pause, she asks: LISA: Are you leaving, too?
ALBERTO: Sì. Vado... in Germania. Devo tenere un ciclo di lezioni in alcune università.	ALBERTO: Yes, I'm going... to Germany. I'm going on a lecture tour there.
[he is lying, too; he is about to undergo surgery to have the bullet removed from his head]	
LISA: Starà via a lungo?	LISA: Are you staying away for long?
ALBERTO: Un mese. Dopo una pausa: Suo padre cosa fa?	ALBERTO: One month. After a pause: What does your father do?
LISA: E' insegnante. Perché?	LISA: He's a teacher. Why?
ALBERTO: Così. Abbozza un sorriso. Poi le alza il cappuccio della giacca: Si copra, si sta bagnando tutta.	ALBERTO: No reason. He attempts a smile. Then he raises the hood of Lisa's coat: Cover your head. It's raining.

LISA: Grazie. Lisa è in imbarazzo.	LISA: Thank you. Lisa is embarrassed.
ALBERTO: Però forse lo faccio solo per educazione. Lei non mi è simpatica.	ALBERTO: Maybe I just did it out of good manners. I don't really like you.
LISA: Pazienza.	LISA: Well, doesn't matter.
Arriva il taxi. Lisa si volta e guarda Alberto: LISA: Bè, allora... Buon viaggio.	The taxi arrives. Lisa turns and looks at Alberto: LISA: Well, then... have a good trip.
ALBERTO: Anche a lei.	ALBERTO: The same to you.
Lisa esita ancora un istante. LISA: Vuole un passaggio?	Lisa hesitates again: LISA: Would you like a lift?
ALBERTO: No, grazie.	ALBERTO: No, thanks.
Lisa gets in. Alberto watches the taxi drive away. He walks off in the rain.	

Like in the sequence when Lisa rings the bell at Alberto's apartment, the two resort to small-talk. This too is a form of involvement, since both show some interest in the other. But, as we have just seen, this final dialogue takes in the eyes of the viewer a decisive turn when Lisa and Alberto both lie about their real destinations – hospital and prison – to avoid embarrassing the other, to save the other's face.

Their sacrifice, which goes unnoticed by the other, means however for Lisa an apology and for Alberto at least the seeds of reluctant forgiveness. Alberto embraces now the possibility of overcoming his trauma, although the surgical operation does entail a risk. Lisa has broken the rules of her program of rehabilitation and will lose the right to work outside, but now she has come out of her limbo by acting as a free and responsible person. When the quite humane parole judge asks her "Was it worth it, at least?", Lisa's answer is "I don't know". The answer is forwarded to the viewer, who did not get the ellipsis explained, but is expected to make sense of her dialogue with Alberto and draw her/his conclusions.

Conclusions

Both the interview with Silveria Russo and the final scenes of La seconda volta show dialogue at work. The actors involved in the talk listen, try to understand and to help the other understand; they are not concerned with themselves only. And in both cases the viewer is not told what he or she is supposed to think. The interviewer and the film director act neither as prosecutors, nor as defence lawyers; this does not mean indifference, but rather a clear choice for internally persuasive against authoritative discourse (Bakhtin, 1981: 342-4).

However, these two examples are the exception more than the rule. It is possible to find other examples of polyphonical and dialogical discourse about political violence in the '70s in Italy, but monological accounts – both fictional or non fictional – are prevalent. Former terrorists' memoirs and fictional autobiographical narratives in particular often have a self-defensive element which tends to become self-referential. But what surprised us was the meagre fictional material available about Italian terrorism and political violence in the '70s: a few films, a few short stories, no notable novels or plays. Not even in fiction Italy seems ready to confront the traumas of its recent past and help a large audience to make sense of what happened. If we look at the non-fictional front, the scene has been dominated by the media's somewhat morbid interest in former terrorists' accounts and memoirs (while for example accounts from the victims are scarce) or by monological statements at the service of one or another position in the political debate.

As to our initial hypothesis, that fiction is in itself more polyphonical and dialogical than non-fiction, we can say that this holds in the case of La Seconda Volta, which manages to give a non-reductive voice to a victim and to an ex-perpetrator, while at the same showing the limitations of leaving the problem of overcoming the past to the judiciary system alone. Here fiction does show its advantage: the freedom to create possible worlds (Bruner, 1986) and to demand that the reader or viewer interpret them by creating new meaning from the text (Eco, 1979).

What's more, by incorporating ellipsis and silence in a plot – that is by refraining from saying things directly and leaving instead the reader or viewer "to do the work" – fiction can offer a privileged path to understanding. In Keith Oatley's words, fiction is "twice as true as facts" because it works as a kind of cognitive and emotional simulation, which allows us to explore our feelings and understandings about a given set of reality (Oatley, 1996).

Nevertheless, we did find dialogue and trust in the reader or viewer's intelligence and sensibility also in Sergio Zavoli's TV program La notte della Repubblica, based on public interviews. We wish to stress, however, that Zavoli's attitude of watchful listening without complicity or hostility has to be considered an exception: refusing to lecture the public and refusing to hurt an opponent is at odds with genre constraints and conventions of public debate in Italy and elsewhere (Calabrese, 1998; Tannen, 1998).

Of course, dialogue does not occur in a vacuum and texts and TV programs alone, be they fictional or documentary, cannot by their sheer power subvert the constraints of hegemonic public discourse. Besides, as noted by Fairclough (2000), dialogue in the public sphere presupposes that participants be able to take action, for example by implementing or influencing policies, as within a 'commission for truth and reconciliation'; but such a hypothesis seems even less viable after the 11th September 2001.

However, the need is still there to understand and overcome a dark period in our recent past, and is possibly more urgent today than ever before, faced with the multiple threats to peace and democracy posed by terrorism and also by the war against it. In March 2002 the Red Brigades, or whoever hides behind this name, killed the economist Marco Biagi, who was cooperating with the right-wing Italian government on labour reform. In a moment when commenting on the crime was embarrassing for all the political forces[14], one of the first public responses to the killing was the prime-time broadcasting of La Seconda Volta on the most popular TV channel. We believe this was a good choice: although fiction can not create dialogue where there is none, a good model is a precious resource.

---

14 The right-wing government had failed to protect him, while the left-wing was campaigning against the labour reforms that Marco Biagi was contributing to shape and defend publicly.

References

Alunni, Corrado 2001. "Introduzione" [foreword]. In Teresa Zoni Zanetti, Clandestina. Rome: DeriveApprodi.

Bakhtin, Mikhhail 1981. "Discourse in the novel." In The dialogic imagination. Four essays by M. M. Bakhtin, M. Holquist (ed) pp. 259-422. Austin: University of Texas Press.

Bakhtin, Mikhhail 1984. Problems of Dostoevsky's poetics. Minneapolis: University of Minnesota Press (Original essays written in 1923 and 1961 according to Todorov 1984).

Bakhtin, Mikhhail 1986. "Toward a methodology for the human sciences." In Speech Genres & Other Late Essays, C. Emerson & M. Holquist (eds) pp. 159-172, Austin: University of Texas Press (Original written in 1974 according to Todorov 1984).

Braghetti Anna Laura & Mambro, Francesca 1995. Nel cerchio della prigione. Milan: Sperling &Kupfer.

Bruner, Jerome 1986. Actual Minds, Possible Worlds. Cambridge, MA: Harvard University Press.

Calabrese, Omar 1998. Come nella boxe. Lo spettacolo della politica in TV. Bari: Laterza.

Chafe, W.L. 1985. "Linguistic differences produced by differences between speaking and writing". In D.R. Olson, N. Torrance, & A. Hildyard (Eds.), Literacy, language and learning: The nature and consequences of reading and writing, pp. 105-123. Cambridge, MA: Cambridge University Press.

Curcio, Renato 1993. A viso aperto. Vita e memori del fondatore delle BR. Intervista di Mario Scialoja. Milan: Mondatori.

De Lutiis, Giuseppe 1996. Il lato oscuro del potere associazioni politiche e strutture paramilitari segrete dal 1946 a oggi. Rome: Editori Riuniti.

Eco, Umberto 1979. The Role of the Reader. Explorations in Semiotics of the Text. Bloomington, IN: Indiana University Press.

Fairclough, Norman 2000. "Dialogue in the public sphere". In Discourse and Social Life, S. Sarangi & M. Coulthard (eds), pp. 170-184.Harlow, England: Longman.

Franceschini, Alberto 1995. Ma io invece voglio parlare. In "L'Unità", 25 ottobre 1995.

O'Leary, Alan 2002. Tragedia all'italiana: Interpreting terrorism and the "anni di piombo" in Italian film. MPhil Dissertation 2002, Wolfson College, Cambridge (unpublished).

Oatley, Keith 1996. Why fiction is twice as true as facts: Fiction as cognitive and emotional simulation. In "Review of General Psychology" 3, pp. 101-117.

Ponti, Nadia 1997. Lettera ai compagni [A letter to the comrades] in: www.ecn.org/rete.sprigionare/italia2.htm (seen 15.10.2002).

Tannen, Deborah 1984. Conversational style: Analyzing talk among friends. Norwood, NJ: Ablex.

Tannen, Deborah 1989. Talking Voices: Repetition, Dialogue and Imagery in Conversational Discourse. Cambridge: Cambridge University Press.

Tannen, Deborah 1992. "How is conversation like literary discourse? The role of imagery and details in creating involvement". In P. Downing, S. D. Lima, and M. Noonan (Eds.), The Linguistics of Literacy, Amsterdam and Philadelphia: John Benjamins, pp. 31-46.

Tannen, Deborah 1997. "Involvement as Dialogue: Linguistic Theory and the Relation Between Conversational and Literary Discourse". In M. Macovski (ed), Dialogue and Critical Discourse, New York and Oxford: Oxford University Press, pp. 137-157.

Tannen, Deborah 1998. The Argument Culture. Changing The Way We Argue and Debate. New York: Random House.

Tarantelli, Carol Beebe 1999. Terrorismo e psicanalisi. In "MicroMega" 3, 1999, pp. 51-71.

Todorov, Tzvetan 1984: Mikhail Bakhtin: The dialogical principle. Translation by Wlad Godzich. Minneapolis: University of Minnesota Press (Ed. orig. 1981, Mikhail Bakhtine. Le principe dialogique. Paris, Éditions du Seuil).

Todorov, Tzvetan. 1982. La conquête de l'Amérique. La question de l'autre, Paris: Éditions du Seuil.

Todorov, Tzvetan. 1991. Face à l'extrême, Paris: Éditions du Seuil.

Todorov, Tzvetan.1995. Une tragédie française. Été 1944: scènes de guerre civile, Paris: Éditions du Seuil.

Zavoli, Sergio 1992. La notte della repubblica, Milan: Mondadori.

SELLING MOZART IN SALZBURG
Multisystemiotic Approach

Eija Ventola

INTRODUCTION

Mozart is a concept that everyone associates with Salzburg, Austria. He was born in Salzburg 27.1.1756 and died in Vienna 5.12.1792. It is generally known that Mozart actually hated living in Salzburg and did not have a high opinion of Salzburg and its bourgeois society. Thus it is somewhat ironical that throughout the times Salzburg has in fact scrupulously used Mozart for its own interests, namely profiting from him – first, as a famous child progeny and composer, and later as a semiotic concept around which it has built a considerable tourist and product industry. Today the city of Salzburg cashes on Mozart and his music through numerous events and objects advertised in his name, and in fact his name and images constitute an essential proportion of the economy of the city.

For a linguist and a semiotician it is interesting to investigate how this selling ideology is construed through various semiotic means, for example, texts, images, souvenirs, etc. of the composer in Salzburg. This paper will look at the various *multisemiotic* ways in which the relationship between Mozart and Salzburg is linguistically and visually construed for the visitors and for the people living in Salzburg. The focus will be on *semiotic commercialising Mozart by using images and products*. The paper suggests that we are here dealing with a *multisystemiotic* meaning-making process of construing our world as visitors or residents around 'Mozart' in Salzburg. The paper will first discuss the developments in systemic-functional linguistics and beyond which have lead to this multisystemiotic approach. It then illustrates how the semiotics of marketization and commercialization already begins in the way Mozart plays a role in *spatial orientation*, when visitors are guided to the city and through various spaces in the city. Further, the focus will be on the kinds of *products* that carry Mozart's images and thus sell products in his name, although they in fact have nothing or very little to do with Mozart and his personality or his music. Finally, the paper argues that this kind of an approach can be useful for educational purposes in instructing students how to approach the data surrounding them multisystemiotically and also critically.

From Multimodality to Multisystemiotics
– A Theory for Exploration of Multisemiotic Meanings in Contexts

Semiotic interests are naturally nothing new (cf. semiotics and research in non-verbal semiotics). Yet it is only relatively recently that linguists have become interested in other semiotic means of meaning-making than language and have started combining language descriptions with semiotic considerations. In other words, the linguistic analyses have been conducted separately from e.g. analyses of pictures. The semiotic analyses of images goes back at least to the significant article of Barthes about the message of the photograph (1961/1984). Hall (1972/1984), following Barthes, suggested ways of analysing pictures in newspapers. But it seems justified to say that for long image semiotics and language semiotics went their separate ways and hardly met. Today, however, the paths do not only cross each other occasionally, they have started running parallel to one another, and even joining up to make a wider interdisciplinary basis for analysing semiotic contexts and semiotic meaing-making.

The major impetus for ways of analysing pictures, sculptures, architecture, film, internet media, etc. within systemic-functional linguistics has been the work of O'Toole (1994), Kress and van Leeuwen (1990, 1996, 2001) and various authors in Baldry (2000) and Baldry and Thibault

(2004). They all have taken the Hallidayan (1994) tri-functional model of language as the basic principal for building up a theory of multimodality and giving analysts appropriate tools for analysing any semiotic material. When looking at language, systemic-functional linguists have always focussed on language patterns that realize three different kinds of functional meanings, e.g. on the lexicogrammatical level *ideational* transitivity patterns, *interpersonal* mood patterns and appraisal realisations, *textual* theme-rheme patterns, etc., and how these patterns are motivated by context of situation (Register) variables Field, Tenor and Mode, and context of culture (Genre) (see e.g. Halliday 1994, Martin 1992, Martin and Rose 2003 and many others). These interests in linguistic patterns and their analyses are in systemic-functional linguistics now expanding to other semiotic codings and their working with language. This multiple view offers us more possibilities of symbiotic analyses of meaning-making in context and also helps us to view and understand how this symbiosis also realizes ideologies in discourse communities. The metafunctional approach in situational and linguistic analysis (i.e. Field/ideational, Tenor/interpersonal and Mode/textual) is now extended to other semiotic systems. Thus, for example Kress and van Leeuwen and O'Toole discuss the ideational function in visuals as e.g. presentational and transactional processes with relevant actors and circumstances, the interpersonal function in terms of 'engagement' through gaze, angle, etc. and compositional function in terms of frames, parallels, verticals, horizontals, diagonals, and so on (for details, see Kress and van Leeuwen 1990, 1996, O'Toole 1994). In *Multimodal Discourse* (2001), Kress and van Leeuwen expand their theoretical views to cover the following areas: discourse, design, production and distribution. This will cover the analysis of discourse from the way texts and visuals are planned to cooperate together, how the discourses are then produced, and how they are made available to their consumers in social and cultural contexts. These extentions of the systemic-functional model have been applied to analyses of multimodal texts, for example, in educational contexts (see Kress et al. 2001; Baldry 2000) and museum contexts (see Ravelli 1996, Purser 2000, Hofinger and Ventola 2004) and in various other contexts (see O'Halloran 2004; Ventola et al 2004), and they have started to influence scholars outside systemic-functional linguistics (see e.g. Scollon & Scollon 2003 and papers in LeVine and Scollon 2004).

This paper will initially draw upon these developments of *the multimodal theory* proposed by the abovementioned systemic-functional linguists. But it also proposes that the theory must be developed further, not just to handle the traditional questions of *Mode*. Very early on a suggestion for a *multisemiotic* approach was proposed in Ventola (1988). The need for this approach was seen in the service encounter contexts, where serious consideration of non-verbal issues was also necessary, but was not at that stage yet largely practised in systemic analyses. Now, it seems that we not only need a *multisemiotic* approach, but a *multisystemiotic* approach. Because, if we are to follow the Firthian principles, we must really even press on further and describe all the many semiotic systems (system networks) that constitute our societies and cultures and the subsequent semiotic structures that realize the choices from these multisemiotic systems. In short, we should always strive for *multisystemiotic explanations and descriptions* of our data and its context. This paper can only point towards some directions of this kind by demonstrating how a *multisystemiotic* theory enables the researcher *to capture the various semiotic realizations concerning marketization and commercialization of Mozart in Salzburg*. These commercialization manifestations are naturally very interesting semiotically and ideologically. They are, practically speaking, used to sell any product. As consumers, therefore, we need to understand these processes and forces of selling and consuming – frequently to protect ourselves from over marketization. Thus we urgently need a comprehensive theory of how texts, images, etc. work in societal contexts between selling products, selling competing products, selling superfluous products, products that may not even in the end be good for us. Analysing today's marketing and consumerism and its effects on people in social contexts demands multisystemiotic analyses.

There is no space here to explain and illustrate the multisystemiotic theory in detail, and even in this limited example context of Mozart and Salzburg no attempt will be made to draw the relevant semiotic system choices. The process of developing such on overarching multisystemiotic theory is still very much in the making, and therefore it is perhaps too early to attempt full descriptions. Yet, it is worthwhile to draw readers' attention to some major areas where such multisemiotic processes operate and suggest that they need to be analysed as multisemiotic systems and structures. It seems that the way Mozart and his image are used by/in Salzburg unscrupulously allows us to study 'Mozart' as a complex semiotic phenomenon in Salzburg and enables us to make students of linguistics and semiotics aware of their surroundings in Salzburg and the commercial ideologies that they live in. The questions raised therefore are e.g.: Is Salzburg selling Mozart and his image – to its extreme? What ideological consequences does such utilization of a personality and its images for various semiotic purposes have and who carries the responsibility, e.g. for an overload in 'Mozart semiotics' due to which the use of Mozart in all fields of life is no longer perceived just positively? When does marketing and consumerism become merely 'bad taste'? The Mozart examples that will be discussed below will illustrate the procedures of hard competition in marketing and advertising. Similar semiotic developments have taken place of course with many other important personalities, for example recently with Lady Diana. Whereas 'selling Mozart' e.g. through chocolates – the most frequent association with Mozart after his music - might today not offend anyone, as chocolates are not considered very serious and harmful products, but the means and ways of selling other personalities, for instance methods of 'selling Lady Di' might be offensive to many. We shall begin this multisystemiotic exploration as if we took a tour in Salzburg; we begin with spatial orientation and then focus on the kind of products that are used in marketing and commercializing Mozart.

Place and Spatial orientation: Cities, Streets, Squares, Buildings, ...

Orientation to places and spaces is organised according to the needs and functions of individuals. Thus accordingly, I as an academic have my orientation to my workplace (which used to be in Salzburg, now in Helsinki). Certain paths (I try to vary them) take me (almost) every day to the university, where I have an office which I have organised according to my own special needs, with a computer in one section, books in another, other technical equipment in another section, a negotiation table for small meetings, and so on. Place organisation I can hardly influence at all, except for varying the route I take to the university. Some of the spatial organisation at the office I can determine, some has already been determined for me. I can shift the furniture around the space, but I cannot shift my office to another building.

When the study of places and spaces goes beyond the common study of linguistic means of expression of, for instance, the grammatical role of a Circumstance (realised e.g. by adverbs and prepositional phrases), then it is new area to linguistics (and maybe also somewhat new to semiotics), but not to citiplanners, architects, interior decorators, organizational managers, etc. There are strong indications that we need more interdisciplinary work in this area, because our discourses do take place in places and spaces, yet we have no overarching theory of how places and spaces influence our discourse realizations. Greatly influenced by the work of Kress and van Leeuwen, Scollon and Scollon (2003) have taken on to develop an approach of analysing places and spaces, which they call *geosemiotics*. To them important in geosemiotics are analyses of *indexicality* (some aspects of the system which in systemic linguistics is identification (reference) in Martin, 1992), *interaction order* (from Goffman referring to recognizable social interactions), *visual semiotics* (the grammar of images as outlined by Kress and van Leeuwen 1996). The central systems for place semiotics are, however, *code preference* (the significance of multilingual signs, e.g. street signs), *inscription* (choice of typesettings, fonts, etc.), *emplacement* (where e.g. the images are placed in the real world). Their approach is probably the closest to the multisystemiotic approach called forth above. The disadvantage of their approach is that it is not developed according to the systematic Firthian and systemic functional principles and thus does not perhaps have the full rigour of a theory that has been called forth. But we have to understand that their work, as the discussion in this paper, is work in progress and both are steps in the process of developing the theory and are intended to take the discussion 'beyond the usual' in linguistics. In fact, much of the work done in contextual discourse analysis could and perhaps should be reinterpreted from this geosemiotic point of view, e.g. many of the examples in my own paper from 1997 (Ventola 1997) could be reinterpreted from this point of view. I am not going to use Scollon and Scollon's term *geosemiotics* in this paper, as I think that if adopted it should be called *geosystemiotics*, and because I am here interested in place and spatial orientation working together with marketization and commercialization. When thinking about Mozart and Salzburg, we may first think about the orientation needs that most visitors have and how the City of Salzburg functions to meet these needs in places and spaces and connects Mozart as a semiotic concept in them.

Official buildings, squares and spaces

When tourists arrive to Salzburg by plane, they immediately meet with 'Mozart' by being welcomed to the *International Salzburg Airport W. A. Mozart*. This is their first encounter with Mozart's name and image of him in their orientation in Salzburg. The second may be when they get a map which helps them with orientation to places in a strange city. When we look at the map of Salzburg, we find *official buildings, squares and spaces* where Mozart again plays a role. All these set an *orientation on Mozart*. There is naturally *Mozart's Geburtshaus* (Mozart's birthplace) and *Mozart's Wohnhaus* (Mozart residence), see Figures 1 and 2. Both of these buildings of course have a history connected with Mozart and his life.

Fig. 2. Mozart's Wohnhaus, Salzburg.

Fig. 1. Mozart's Geburtshaus, Salzburg.

The tourist also finds various other official buildings and places in the city that are connected with Mozart's name, but have no direct link with his history, e.g. *Mozarteum* is the Music School, but was of course never visited by Mozart. In the centre of the city there is *Mozartplatz*, on which we find a *statue of Mozart*, see Figure 3.

Fig. 3. The statue of Mozart on Mozartplatz, Salzburg.

Commercial buildings, squares and spaces

The focus has so far been on the official buildings which orient the visitor to Mozart as a semiotic concept in Salzburg. But in addition to these official buildings, Mozart is also used by numerous *commercial buildings, squares and spaces* which enhance the visitors' orientation to the role of Mozart in Salzburg as a semiotic construal.

Fig. 4. Hotel Amadeus, Salzburg.

Fig. 5. Shirt Shop zum Mozart, Salzburg.   Fig. 6. Reber Chocolate Shop, Salzburg.

Within the commercial spaces, we may also find that there are *special sections* which also semiotically orient the visitor to Mozart, and of course the products associated with Mozart (discussed in detail in Section 4). An example given here is a local corner shop, *Spar*, in which we find a section that is devoted to Mozart products – liqueurs and chocolates (see Figures 7, 8 and 9).

Fig. 7. A local Spar shop, Salzburg.

Fig. 8. The liqueur section in the Spar.   Fig. 9. The chocolate section in the Spar shop.

To summarize this section, then, the official and commercial buildings, squares and spaces give an official status and justification to the use of *Mozart* in marketization and commercialization in Salzburg, and they add to the semiotic interpretation of Mozart and his life in Salzburg through his name and images that are used throughout the city to promote the city and it products (i.e. earn the city money). The next section will deal with the orientation to Mozart through the range of products that are sold throughout Salzburg.

Range of Products

Mozart sells – not just in the field of music but in various other fields in Salzburg. His name or images thus *reinforce* the connection between Salzburg and Mozart through various products. In the field of *music*, there are of course the CDs, cassettes, and concerts that perform his music. But Salzburg not only sells Mozart's music but also its *gastronomy* through Mozart. Thus, a tourist can book to attend a *Mozart Dinner Concert*:

> A seduction in music and culinary arts in the stylish ambiance of the historic Baroque hall in the Stiftskeller St. Peter restaurant. Enjoy the most popular compositions by W. A. Mozart by candlelight – with music played by Salzburg artists in historic costumes – and a multiple-course dinner, prepared according to traditional recipes from the 17th and 18th centuries. (from the advertising brochure)

Another competing dinner in the Fortress of Hohensalzburg, the castle that rules over Salzburg on a hill, is advertised as "a culinary-musical experience over the rooftops of Salzburg" (from the advertising brochure). The Stiftskeller brochure does not actually use the image of Mozart for selling the dinner concert whereas the Fortress brochure does. In the field of *eating and drinking* we naturally have to mention the 'Mozart liqueurs' (see Figure 8) and the 'Mozart chocolates' (see Figure 9), which will also be discussed in more detail later in this section.

As far as *clothing* is concerned, one can find, for instance, Mozart T-shirts (either with his image, name or music on them), Mozart socks,

Mozart umbrellas. In the field of *household goods* there are various kinds of Mozart glasses, plates and cups, many of these are intended merely for decorative purposes only, though. One can take care of one's *personal hygiene* also with Mozart products: Mozart shampoo, Mozart perfume, Amadeus perfume, etc. For *writing* there are not only postcards, but also notepads, pens, pencils, erasers, and there are many different kinds of additional *souvenirs* that one can take back home to relatives and friends from Salzburg: playing cards, magnets, dolls, and so on. Some of these items can be seen in Figure 10.

The range of products gives an impression of the way that Salzburg 'cashes in' with Mozart in its commerce. If suddenly the shop keepers and the manufacturers were denied the right of using Mozart's name, they would be utterly shocked. Let us take one product specifically under scrutiny, and we shall see how hard the competition can be, also semiotically.

One of the products that has also become a 'sign' for Salzburg and Mozart is the *Mozartkugel*, a round chocolate ball, which has various layers. The history of the 'Kugel' is displayed in a shop in the centre of Salzburg. This Kugel, with its silver wrapping but with no picture of Mozart, is according to this text the *original* one.

> The Salzburg confectioner, PAUL FÜRST, created the now world famous Salzburger Mozartkugel in the year 1890. He was awarded a gold medal for his product, which had already become famous, at the Paris Exhibition of 1905. NORBERT FÜRST, the present proprietor of this establishment [the shop], still makes these fine chocolates today according to the old recipe and method handed down to him by his greatgrandfather. For this reason, these can truly be called ORIGINAL SALZBURGER MOZARTKUGEL.

The competition however is great. The Mirabell company in Salzburg has opted for mass production and markets its Kugel as 'Echte Salzburger Mozartkugeln' (Authentic Salzburger Mozartkugeln). It uses the image of Mozart both in its Kugel chocolate boxes as well as in the golden wrappings of the chocolates. Somewhat apologetically it explains that due to

Figure 10. Various Mozart items for sale in Salzburg.

large demand it has had to give up the traditional method of producing the Kugel.

> The history of a world famous composition.
> The history of the Mozartkugel began – it almost goes without saying – in the place where the ingenious composer W. A. Mozart was born in 1756: in Salzburg. In 1890, the Salzburg confectioner Paul Fürst, a master of his art, created the Mozartkugel. He shaped a ball of marzipan, rolled it in nougat cream and speared it with a tiny wooden stick. Afterwards, he dipped it into bitter-sweet chocolate. Even today, Mozartkugeln are being produced in the "Konditorei Fürst" in Salzburg. The Salzburg company Mirabell also used to produce their Echte Salzburger Mozartkugeln by hand according to the Mozartkugel tradition. In order to meet the growing consumer demand, this laborious manual process was later developed into industrial production. In the course of the years, Mirabell's Echte Salzburger Mozartkugeln in their unmistakable, red-and-golden octagonal box became one of the most famous confectionary specialities. Today, they are a popular gift, a most typical Austrian souvenir and a synonym for Austria all around the globe. (from a Mirabell Salzburger Mozartkugeln advertisement)

The text and the image cleverly links Mozart to the Kugel with the semantic link *composition* and with the image of Mozart. The Echte Salzburger Mozartkugeln and their typical box are seen in Figure 11 on the right, and on the left we have a Viennese competition to the Salzburger Mozartkugeln. Notice that the images of Mozart on the Kugel and the boxes are different.

The image of Mozart is again different in the Mozartkugel produced by the Reber company in Bad Reichenhall, the neighbouring German town in Bavaria. The presence of Reber company is also prominent in the streets of Salzburg, because Reber has established special shops in which the Reber Mozartkugeln are sold. The Salzburg newspaper, the Salzburger Nachrichten, recently reported that not the Fürst nor the Mirabell company, but the Reber company will actually be the main sponsor for the Mozart exhibition in 2006, organized to celebrate his 250th birthday. Figure 12 shows one of these Reber shops in Salzburg and

Figure 13 shows the image of Mozart that is used by the Reber company in their advertisements. In addition to the Mozartkugel mentioned so far, there are at lest two or three other companies that sell their chocolates with the name and image of Mozart.

Figure 11. A Viennese and a Salzburger Mozartkugel box.

Figure 12. A Reber shop in Salzburg.

Figure 13. An enlarged picture of the Mozart image used by the Reber shop.

Multisystemiotics – useful for exploring semiotic spanning

So far, the purpose of the paper has been to demonstrate what a complex semiotic phenomenon Mozart has actually become in Salzburg. The marketing and commercialization methods are naturally interesting to all of us – they make us understand our world better semiotically and ideologically. Although this paper, due to reasons of space (and for reasons explained in Section 2) will not carry out detailed analyses all the examples (and many more which exist in Salzburg), it is claimed that multisystemiotic analyses will enable us to perceive how discourses are planned to cooperate together or link up with other texts, visuals, etc., how these multisystemiotic discourses are produced, and how they are distributed to consumers in social and cultural contexts and the effects they have.

We can start to get an idea how this kind of a theory may operate when we attempt to analyse, for example, the way Mozart images are utilized in various kinds of discourses in Salzburg. Figures 14 and 15 will function as examples.

Fig. 14. The image of Mozart in two post cards.

Fig. 15. The Mozart statue in an advertisement.

The images in the two postcards in Figure 14 are slightly different, but ideationally they represent the same meanings. Mozart seems to be only posing as a model for the painter of the picture, i.e. he is merely 'represented' and is no way involved in action. But this is only the representation in these postcards. It may be that in the original picture Mozart might actually be playing the piano; in other words, the process would be transactional. In both pictures his gaze is directed to the viewer, and he thus engages the viewer. But this gaze is compositionally framed in both pictures in quite a different manner. On the postcard on the left, Mozart is definitely the major figure, although the violin and his signature are set in the foreground and can thus be considered to highlight the recognition of why this figure in the postcard is important (cf. the interpretation of the theme in the clauses as the sayer's 'this is what I am on about'). On the postcard on the right, Mozart is in the centre and is also foregrounded, but around him are then images of the sights of Salzburg. Although Mozart is the major image, the message of the postcard may be interpreted as

'Mozart is one aspect of Salzburg'. So compositionally, these images of Mozart work in a different way in these postcards. We can say that here we have an example of *semiotic spanning*, the way of using language and/or images for purposes of meaning-making other than those intended in the original context (for a discussion, see Ventola 1999, 2002). Language and images are transferred from the original context for other meaning-making purposes, frequently for ideological purposes.

In Figure 15, we can see how the Salzburger Nachrichten uses the Mozart statue for marketing purposes through semiotic spanning. Semiotic spanning in advertising was also used throughout Salzburg on many of the city buses, when I lived there. Both sides of the buses carried an advertisement of the Echte Salzburger Kugel. Thus the image of Mozart was transferred from the original painting to the Kugel advertisement and further to the advertising spaces on the buses.

Conclusion

This paper has focussed on Mozart and how Salzburg has marketed him semiotically. His name and image have become the most successful product that Salzburg has to sell, and Salzburg makes full use of this selling potential of Mozart. We can speak of accumulation of marketisation and commercialisation through the process of semiotic spanning – the theory of systemiotics will hopefully in the future capture more precisely how this happens and help us to deal with this kind of meaning-making critically, so that we can develop a critical attitude to various ideologies that are prominent in marketing. This is the answer to the question 'what do we need this kind of theory for?' For any individual it is of vital importance to study one's own environment, in order to function in it appropriately and to deal critically with it. Students of foreign languages must learn the tools for doing semiotic analysis (both linguistic and non-linguistic). They have to be able to analyse both their native languages and their own cultures and the foreign language and the foreign cultural contexts they are teaching. They must be aware of the different means of meaning-making and where possibly the systems clash. If they live in a place like Salzburg, an international tourist city, they can observe linguistic and cultural realisations in many languages, and they will also perceive frequent linguistic and cultural clashes. Guiding students to analyse their surroundings and work out the ideologies that are in operation in their own cultures (in this case using Mozart for selling and marketing) hopefully makes them more sensitive to how semiotic systems code meanings in other cultures. By analysing many of these partly trivial places, pictures, texts, and their meanings, students get to practise working with multimodal analyses in their own social contexts. Their immediate surroundings offer them many opportunities to work with real data, and, through the analyses, they learn the kind of ideologies that are in operation around them in society. But naturally, our multisystemiotic theory and tools for analyses still need further sharpening and developing. The work is only just beginning.

REFERENCES

Baldry, A. (ed.) 2000. *Multimodality and Multimediality*. Campobasso: Palladino Editore.

Baldry, A. and P. J. Thibault 2004. *Multimodal Transcription and Text Analysis*. London: Equinox.

Barthes, R. 1961/1984. "Sanoma valokuvassa (Le message photographique)". In *Kuvista sanoin 2*, Lintunen, M. (ed.), 120-137, Porvoo: Suomen valokuvataiteen museon säätiö.

Hall, S. 1972/1984. "Uutikuvien määräytymisprosessi (The determinations on News photographs)". In *Kuvista sanoin 2*, Lintunen, M. (ed.), 138-190, Porvoo: Suomen valokuvataiteen museon säätiö.

Halliday, M. A. K. 1994. *Introduction to Functinal Grammar*. London: Arnold

Hofinger, A. and E. Ventola 2004. In: *Perspectives on Multimodalitz*. E. Ventola, Cassily Charles and M. Kaltenbacher (eds). Amsterdam: Benjamins, 193- 210.

Kress, G. and van Leeuwen, T. 1990. *Reading Images*. Geelong, Vic.: Deakin University.

Kress, G. and van Leeuwen, T. 1996. *Reading Images. The Grammar of Visual Design*. London/NY: Routledge.

Kress, G. and van Leeuwen, T. 2001. *Multimodal Discourse. The Modes and Media of Contemporary Communication*. London: Arnold.

Kress, G. C. Jewitt, J. Ogborn, and C. Tsatsarelis 2001. *Multimodal Teaching and Learning*. London: Continuum.

LeVine, P. and R. Scollon (eds.) 2004. *Discourse and Technology*. Washington, D.C.: Geroegetown University Press.

Martin, J. R. 1992. *English Text. System and Structure.* Amsterdam: Benjamins.

Martin, J. R. and David Rose 2003. *Working with Discourse.* London: Continuum.

O'Halloran, K. (ed.) 2004. *Multimodal Discourse Analysis. Systemic Functional Perspectives.* London: Continuum

O'Toole, M. 1994. *The Language of Displayed Art.* London: Leicester University Press.

Purser, E. 2000. "Telling Stories: text analysis in a museum". In *Discourse and Community: Doing Functional Linguistics,* E. Ventola (ed.), 169-198. Tübingen: Narr.

Ravelli, L. 1996. "Making language accessible: successful text writing for museum visitors". *Linguistics and Education* 8: 367-387.

Scollon, R. & S. Wong Scollon 2003. *Discourses in Place. Language in the Material World.* London: Routledge.

Ventola, E. 1988. "Text Analysis in Operation: A Multilevel Approach." In: Robin P. Fawcett & David Young (eds.). New Developments in Systemic Linguistics, Volume II. London: Pinter, 52-77.

Ventola, E. 1997. "Pendel des sprachlichen Handelns: Funktional linguistische Perspektive. " In: W. Kindermann, (ed.). *Entwicklungslinien: 120 Jahre Anglistik in Halle.* (Hallenser Studien zur Anglistik und Amerikanistik, 2.Münster: LIT Verlag, 211-230.

Ventola, E. 1999. "Semiotic Spanning at Conferences: Cohesion and Coherence in and across conference papers and their discussions". In *Coherence in Spoken and Written Discourse. How to create it and how to describe it.* W. Bublitz, U. Lenk, & E. Ventola, (eds.), 101-125, Amsterdam: Benjamins.

Ventola, E. 2002. "Why and what kind of focus on conference presentations?". In *Conference Language.* E. Ventola, C. Shalom and S. Thompson (eds.), 15-50, Frankfurt am Main: Peter Lang.

Ventola, E., C. Charles and M. Kaltenbacher (eds.) 2004. *Perspectives in Multimodality.* Amsterdam: Benjamins.

POLITICAL DISCOURSE IN THE FEMININE MANIFESTATION
Social Identity
(Queen Marianna of Spain and Governor Roseana of Maranhão)[1]

Dina Maria Martins Ferreira

INITIAL REMARKS

The present set of themes deals with the relationship between the historical space of the objective world and that established in discursive media language as a constructive identity-promoting factor of the feminine manifestation; it shows how feminine attributes meet and touch situated in their multifaceted historicalness, and raises the issue of whether the steadiness and repetition of attributes allocated at each historical moment can be condensed in a macrosphere representative of the human condition in the feminine universe.

In the study of the relationships between histories, the media discourse on the feminine manifestation in politics is selected – a syncretical discourse (both verbal and nonverbal) but with an analytical focus basically on iconicity. The analytical corpus was published in Folha de São Paulo, a newspaper issued nationwide, on March 10, 2002, section A, page 14, in an article by Elio Gaspari entitled "The witches of gross behavior against Roseana Sarney". It is a collage of a painting by the Spanish painter Diego Velásquez – a portrait of Queen Marianna of Spain – from the 17th century, where Roseana's face replaces the Queen's. Marianna's. Roseana

---

1 Translator: Odila da Silveira Jambor

depicts the power validated by the Queen's nobility. Both the histories and the discourse genres coincide: the 21st century of the media reaches the 17th century of the arts, 'prattling away' about feminine power; the media and pictorial discourse intermingle in form on behalf of a complex content identity.

The presuppositions put here will be presented by coverage; notwithstanding, this coverage does not intend to decrease the analytical systematicity. My intention is to build a road that crosses the area of Pragmatics and Semiotics, demonstrating that the object of analysis is the manager of the theoretical presuppositions, which are rendered instrumental in the composition of a reading of the political sense established in the media

Governor Roseane Sarney of Maranhão

Queen Marianne of Spain

discourse at stake. Pragmatics subsidizes an interpretation of the political intentions of a specific discourse, while Semiotics distinguishes the sense of forms that establish contents. Pragmatics and Semiotics will be dealt with as areas that complement each other in analytical readings, whose confluence is not expressed by a paradox, but by harmony.

This choice would entail the adoption of an ideological stance which considers that theory is at the service of the object to be researched. On the contrary, theory will direct the reading of the object to be researched. What I mean is that the analytical interpretation is situated in two directions, the metaphorical direction and the metonymical one. In the former, the object is further from the consideration of the analyst and this distance renders systematicity difficult but broadens the vision of the 'site' where the object moves, for it offers polysemic visions. Therefore, you can say that the distance between the theoretical component and the object to be analysed 'conceals'— but does not wipe out— the theoretical component in the mist of the object's political performance, hampering the systematization required by science.

In the fulfillment of scientific grounding, the metonymical position is often chosen, that is to say, the object is situated close to the analytical eyes of the researcher, who examines singled out forms, which work for the systematization of the analysis. Having chosen this two-tier topology, I dare say that the methodology of this paper responds to the theoretical and conceptual approaches which are built in a construct, organizing and transforming them in favor of the telescopic position chosen.

The theory/methodology combination in/for a construct configures the objective of this paper: the analysis of a historical-political object on the identity of the feminine component, which enables the overflowing of the possibility of the convergence of theoretical positions.

A HISTORICAL-POLITICAL DISCOURSE

Some historical notations are pertinent not only for the intended argumentation, but for the interpretation of the significative reason for this collage, whose narrative organization is in relation to the political component.

Marianna (Maria Anna) of Austria was the daughter of Ferdinand III and Maria of Austria, who, in turn, was the sister of Phillip IV, king of Spain, a widower with no children who had to get married again to provide a heir for the throne. Marianna and Phillip got married and had six children. Among them was Charles II, the last king of Spain of the Habsburg dynasty (the Austrians). Queen Marianna's political importance lies in the fact that with the death of Phillip IV, his son, Charles II, rose to the throne when he was only four years old. Regency Council is established (1665-1675/77), in which Queen Marianna played an important role in a period reigned by political strife. Roseana Sarney, daughter of former president of Brazil José Sarney (1985/89) and, currently (2002) a senator, was, then, the governor of Maranhão, a state in Northeastern Brazil. Her brother, José Sarney Filho, representative and former minister also participates in the political scenario. She is married to Jorge Murad, also a politician, for he renders political consulting services to the Sarney family. In short, Roseana is an active member of a family engaged in politics, called the Sarney oligarchy because it has been castled in the Maranhão tower for 35 years. The thematic focus of these data converge to political scandal: the first feminine figure to reach the prenomination period for the presidency of Brazil, with high public ratings and involved in possible fraud, in partnership with her husband, in her business Lunus Representações e Serviços Ltda [Lunus Representations and Services Ltd.], where R$1.34 million[2] in money were found on a desk in the office.

Historical data will serve as an anchor for the sense proposed by the image. The two woman figures crisscross, that is to say, are established superimposed in the expressiveness of values shared by the feminine manifestation. Marianna and Roseana live within a specific space and time; however, they seem to be linked by a similar property; they seem to meet in *illo tempore* without denying their *temporis* – not only experienced but being experienced. Both, in their sociocultural specificities, are instituted in political power, play an important role in their environment, promote

---

2 *Real (R$)* is the name of the Brazilian currency. In 2004, one dollar is worth approximately R$3,00.

agreements of political interest to their 'empires,' plot on the throne of power, and practice the art of power in their polis.

The feminine manifestation in the semiotic, pragmaticist and symbolic dimensions

The issue of the identity of the feminine manifestation will organize itself along the semiotics, pragmatism and mythological symbolism analytical axis. These axes seek to compare the identity-promoting construct of the feminine manifestation from the point of view of sense-generating modes, of superposed historical performatives, and of ahistorical 'duration' of the mythical meaning. The epistemological convergence strives to neutralize theoretical borderline forces which start to interact in argumentative language games.

On the pragmaticist outlook

Pragmaticist philosophy, of postmetaphysical nature, is grounded on antiessentialism and antirepresentationalism since it does not grant access to the Being and to the Truth. The Truth is reduced to momentary utility; a being does not represent the essence of the Being; he/she only validates a subject in a useful situation. Under the shield of action, Pragmaticism favors "the contingency of the community, language and individuality." (Huisman, 2001: 837). The absolute of essence and truth is dissipated in the contingency of performative moments; that which signifies and/or is signified is the utilitarianism of the action at issue, contextualized in a specific sociohistorical moment.

And from the viewpoint of Pragmaticism, the image expressed – a Velásquez painting with a collage – would be "a historical phenomenon of mirror-imagery, the story of the domination of the mind of the West by ocular metaphors within a social perspective." (Rorty, 1995: 27). Doubtlessly, the 'adulterated' picture represents a historical phenomenon: the figure of a woman that can be called 'Marianna Sarney'(a symbiosis of Marianna of Austria and Roseana Sarney), in magnificent full dress, which demonstrates her social status: that of someone important, who commands and moves under the spotlight of power. In the contingency of the Brazilian social community, there is a coupling of performative data of two feminine figures in two different historical routes, which reflect similar sociocultural value attributions, that is, values of power and frauds ensuing from their practice in the time and space they emerge from.

ON THE SEMIOTIC READING

While Pragmaticism is linked to that which is being signified as action, Semiotics values ways and forms of sense, i.e., it studies language instruments triggered in sense production. The semiotic interpretation proposed is in relation to a theory taking into account means of producing sense. Understood as a study of taxonomic relationships in sense production, Semiotics, in principle, proposes an elementary structure of meanings with their representational systems. Offering such mechanisms, which configure representations, it benefits the metaphysical world of essentialist philosophy.

And under this structuralist interspersion, a semiotic reading of the 'royal' faces indicates the route of discursive signifiers. In the original Velásquez painting, Queen Marianna reflects power in her traits: her lips, eyebrows and eyes rest horizontally, position indicating the stability of power, reassured on principle by the nobility of her family tree itself; her closed lips deny the simplicity of the pathos in human nature; her stern look is indifferent to the spectator; posing for a picture, she expresses the practice of power – I'm here in my tower – power tangled in lace and other feminine trimmings and established in the grandiose decoration of silk curtains, drawn to make room for the powerful court figure. Replacing Marianna's face with Roseana's continues the making of power; it does not interrupt the presence of this category. However, her traits hyperbolize this practice and render it modal: they land in her magnitude, on her lips and eyes; her eyebrows droop dysphorically; euphoric color makes way to black and white; a figure still surrounded by the femininity of lace, indicating, notwithstanding, the need to have weapons behind her in an upright position indicating readiness for combat.

Towards the harmonic collision between Semiotics and Pragmatism

The discursive differences are ratified even with the overlapping of feminine figures, for historical contingency, as its own nature indicates, is specific to its time and space. The portrait of Marianna of Austria is a color portrait; hereditary power is strong in its colors; it is 'royal' due to its genealogical tree and the magnificence of the attire; the Queen's look and attitude indicate the distance between the one that exerts power before those who are under this power; the rich silk of the curtain frames the royal altar. The portrait of 'Marianna Sarney' reveals a Roseana in black and white, discolored and haggard on her pedestal: maybe the feminine manifestation cannot bear power intrigues; it needs weapons to support it since silk cannot bear its weight. In spite of appropriating itself of someone else's social contingency, one historical performative is different from the other.

Nevertheless, the power category remains, independent of the change in form; the signified is stabilized in signifiers in different histories that are joined by the steadiness and repetition of semantic traits constitutive of the signified <power>.The issue is rendered problematic. The portrait of 'Marianna Sarney' aggregates, in its political instant, different times and spaces from the present and past, rebuilding and transforming power endurance. Signifiers move within the resilience of historical times. The <power> construct starts to reveal the historical nonborders, which embrace each other in the cyclic making of the human condition. The signified is prior to the signifier; the signified is deposited in language, whose signifiers glide in its histories. Contradicting postanalytical pragmatism, the representational meaning of power is set up somehow in overlapping feminine figures. Refuting antirepresentationalism, it is associated with antiessentialism since representation does not reflect the essence of power itself. Representation may be considered as an atom of the essence, as a form which manifests itself in the instant of a historical moment. In the capacity of portrait, it is already a representation of something and, insofar as language is accepted as the representation of the world, the photograph represents (in language) the representation of a figure (in a portrait), a superposition resource of representations which already indicates distancing from the essence focus.

Even with the proposal of what language represents, the action of the utilitarian aspect is not denied: to denounce and speak ironically of the feminine practice of power in a social-historical phenomenon. The action takes place, but couldn't the performative aspect and a multiplicity of others represent life data? Doesn't discursive practice mirror representations of social phenomena? Couldn't there be incoherency in the constitution of figures constructed in discourse? How can a woman of the seventeenth correspond to a woman of the 21st century? The sense would not lie in the contradiction, but in the acceptance of the contradiction. It does not matter if the locks in her hair and trimmings in fashion in that 'primeval' century do not match the present face; it does not matter if the feminine figure of the 17th century wears a long stiff skirt, whereas the woman of the present is the one in slacks or a suit; there is no contradiction if the handkerchief gliding along her skirt shows the hierarchical superiority of an age, but not of the present age, and it does not matter if Marianna of Austria is recognized by the newspaper reader or not. The use of that image means that the historical performative of the power plot works and suits the sense: significative making showing "the witches of gross behavior against Roseana Sarney," which, actually and maybe were not only 'gross behavior against her,' but her gross behavior. The meaningful 'expression' is in relation to the way I see form:

> "(the supremacy of form) a position of principle, of faith – since, any example of use that can be discovered after the identification of a certain form and later on be considered as a counterexample of the principle will be a reason not for the principle to be revised, but for the form to be reconsidered (to become aware of the new rebellious datum)" (Rajagopalan, gone to press: p. 8)

The canvas that was tampered with is merely a new use of iconic language indicative of a 'new' form of facing the political phenomenon. The construction of the meaning fulfills the discursive use, for it is accepted, published, and interpreted. If "language is form put into action and every social action is full of unforeseeableness" (Rajagopalan, gone to press: p. 10), the collage made on Velásquez's canvas can be considered an illustration of the unforeseeableness of social action that manifests itself in discursive form.

Still in the world of pragmatism, one could wonder if the canvas by Velásquez with the face of Roseana Sarney constitutes an individual or a culture's public representamen. For their knowledge of the world, one can recognize the individual Queen Marianna of Spain, mother of Charles II, imperial regent, manipulator of political plots and the individual Roseana Sarney, then prenominee to the presidency of Brazil. Without the pretentiousness of being a "radical societalist" (Rajagopalan, under revision: p.2), in other words, without denying what is private, one cannot help recognizing what is collective as the substratum in the identity constitution of Roseana Sarney in that social-historical instant. The individual Roseana Sarney is one who " has no other individuality besides the one that is granted her by the social order she is part of" (Rajagopalan, under revision: p.2), that is, in that language game, in the construction of that meaning, her identity is granted by her social roles.

Private and public intermingle by means of the social factors attributed to an individual (Queen Marianna) who builds the identity of another individual (Roseana) who, in turn, reflects social attributes. Therefore, I propose the institution of a private socializing subject, or, rather a private-collective subject.

THE FEMININE MANIFESTATION IN MYTHICAL SYMBOLISM, THE CONVERGENCE BETWEEN SEMIOTICS AND PRAGMATISM

And it is by the coming together and equivalence of social attributes belonging to distant historical moments that I have kept to the study of identity, in this case, that of the feminine manifestation, which can cope with issues like how historical moments experienced can touch in the ahistorical plan. The mythical symbology universe provides us with resources no longer utilitarian of that instant, but a world that affords an expression of the human condition and its properties, which manifest themselves in histories – beyond the very nature of myth, being understood as stories that epiphanize the 'permanent' truths of life.

The story of Roseana Sarney indicates mythical paths showing the paths of life. She is a woman, and as a woman she rose to the power of a prenomination for the presidency of Brazil; her images always show a feminine figure who pays attention to her appearance, who wears colorful clothes, whose hair is always neatly combed and who is always smiling. Roseana was the first woman at the highest level of federal government. Nevertheless, she was deprived of power by the makings of a man, her husband. This scenario depicts repetitions of life, the sense of life which does not end at the sociocultural borders; there is an expression of endurance in the mythical-symbolic dimension.

It is necessary to understand the concept of endurance, which does not meet essence or finitude-related issues. Even accepting the finitude of that which is pragmatic, finitude cannot be compared to symbolic-mythical 'infinitude,' for there is no infinitude either in myth or in its symbolic manifestation. The standing of the symbolic manifestation is that of nontransparency, a trait that renders it impossible to establish its borders. Conceptualizing mythical symbology through rationalism and/or epistemological positivism is unfeasible even because of its very nature of eidolon, mist that lightly touches social and individual subjects, symbols that simultaneously cover and participate in the tangible part experienced.

A tertium quid is presented because the nonspatial and nontemporal components (indicators of a higher concept of human condition) manifest themselves in the spatial component of a temporal human being. Human 'endurance' is expressed by the nonendurance of contingency.

I dared to conceptualize anew, so to say, in order to grant further justification to the argumentative proposal. I will use the term property as signs of that which is 'characteristic' of human nature, and attributes as social predications that are harnessed to individuals in their social lives. Consequently, I will be working with the social component and human condition: the social component reflects the concreteness of that which promotes identity in its historical-cultural context and human condition, which shows an abstract but not less real universe.

It is through the 'play together with' of ambivalence between instant and endurance that the title of the article is expanded to Athena/Hera of the Olympus, Marianna of Austria and Roseana of Maranhão, insofar as feminine mythological figures from the cradle of Western civilization provide us with archetypal builders of feminine identity in the constitutive journey of life.

The choice of the Greek goddess Athena is made by her hierarchical importance in Greek mythology and mainly because she embodies the symbol of women in power, of a woman who at her birth sprang forth from the head of Zeus without feminine conspiracy, who commands and administers great epic sagas. Athena is the "guardian of the acropolises, a warrior goddess, goddess of wisdom, goddess of reason and of Apollonian balance" (Brandão, 1986: 26). Hera is taken into account as a woman, the 'first lady' of the Olympus on official duty, whose performative aspect is based on backstage plotting, since, in the maintenance of her role as wife of 'King' Zeus, she needs to establish agreements, and scheme frauds to be able to keep her topoi.

Both goddesses become, here on this paper, a historical unit of attributes, so that their attributes can be related to those of Marianna of Austria and Roseana of Maranhão. Athena unveils the political women from the palladium, those who manage cities, women who reflect over politics. These identity-promoting attributes are joined by others pertaining to Hera, a woman who plots and who is always involved in a network of intrigue. Polis and political plotting come together. Once again, historically situated attributes are equivalent: Hera/Athena of the Olympus meets Marianna in Spain, who meets Roseana in Maranhão.

Sharing repeated attributes, feminine figures emanate the steadiness of properties derived from a social performative, to which roles are bequeathed.

In this paper, mythical symbology will not be dealt with in its primeval sense, in which it was formed by ritual and that which is sacralized. Barthes (1973) simplifies the concept of myth so as to adjust it to its manifestation in modern societies. Myth speaks through symbols, presented as a "replaceable form of truth, a truth that purloins another truth." (apud Brandão, 1986: 37) For that matter, myth does not propose to show the essence per se either. It could, then, be understood as "the identity of all men, irrespective of the time and place where they lived." (apud Brandão, 1986: 37) Mircea Eliade (apud Brandão, 1986: 40) says that myth is

> "An object or an act (that) do not become real, unless to the extent that they repeat an archetype. Accordingly, reality is acquired exclusively by repetition or participation; everything that lacks an exemplar model is void of sense, that is to say, lacks reality."

What happens in/through feminine figures created in discourse is the steadiness of the property that manifests itself through historical functions. They share the power property and the political strategy skill. By the repetition of attributes, social performatives, one can perceive categories of human condition. Human properties live with social attributes; histories reveal ahistory. The manifestation of language in a specific instant is the epiphanic channel of human properties.

Conclusion

The mythical and pragmaticist world, apparently divergent, touch through the 'manner manifested,' a transfer vein between one universe and the other, since symbology is not "an object, a concept or an idea: it is a variation of the sense, a form" (Barthes, 1970: 13, apud Brandão, 1987). Quoting the philosopher Quine, I call the endurance of human condition "to be is to be the value of a variation" (apud Rajagopalan, 2000:80), owing to the fact that the "being" is shown in constitutive performativity in a social "variation" reflecting a "value" of the sense of "being."

Neither the pragmaticist nor the symbolical-mythical universe permits attaining the essence of being, but the epiphany of values (properties of the human condition) is presented by means of variations (social-historical attributes). The construct is not undone by the steadiness of the values. The steadiness and repetition of the historical component allows a glimpse of ethereal values of the human condition which have touched us lightly since and beyond illo tempore. The repetition of makings in the order of pragmaticist contingency leaves traces, traces of the existence of the human condition. The language is ecological, and, as such, it leaves traces of historical senses of other histories, whose continuity propitiates an illo tempore expression. Pragmatism and mythology are not epistemic dichotomies; a tertium quid is possible: interhistories sow ahistory; pragmatisms render mythologies epiphanic.

Through the knowledge of this combination of universes – properties and attributes – epistemology does not award itself a certificate for the success in the discovery of the truth in life; this knowledge only "will give us something to go on." (Rorty 1996: 249).

REFERENCES

Barthes, R. , 1973, Mitologias (Mythologies) , Lisboa, Edições 70.

Brandão, J. de S,1986, Mitologia Grega, (Greek Mythology), Volume I, Rio de Janeiro, Vozes.

Brandão. J. de S., 1987, Mitologia Grega, (Greek Mythology),Volume II, Rio de Janeiro, Vozes.

Eliade, M., 1996, Imagens e Símbolos. Ensaio sobre o simbolismo mágico-religioso,

(Images and Symbols. Essay on magic-religious symbolism), São Paulo, Martins Fontes.

Greimas, A.J. e Courtès, J., 1989, Dicionário de Semiótica, (Semiotics Dictionary) São Paulo, Cultrix.

Huisman, D. (2001), Dicionário dos Filósofos, (The Philosophers' Dictionary)

São Paulo, Martins Fontes.

Rajagopalan, K., gone to press, Por uma pragmática voltada à prática lingüística, (For a Pragmatics aimed at linguistic practice) In: Zandwais, A. (orga.), A relação entre

Pragmática e Enunciação, (The relationship between Pragmatics and the manner of expression), UFRGS [Universidade Federal do Rio Grande do Sul/The Federal University of the State of Rio Grande do Sul].

Rajagopalan, K., under revision, A teoria pragmática e a necessidade de considerar o sujeito da linguagem como um agente ético, (Pragmatic theory and the need to consider the language subject as an ethical agent)

Rajagopalan, K., 2000, O singular: uma pedra no caminho dos teóricos da linguagem, (Uniqueness: a hindrance in the path of language theoreticians)Cadernos de Estudos da Linguagem (Books on Language Studies), N° 38, pp.79-84.

Rorty, R., 1979, Philosophy and the Mirror of Nature, Princeton, New Jersey, Princeton University Press.